W9-CDU-938

PEACEFUL LIVING
IN A
STRESSFUL
WORLD

PEACEFUL LIVING
IN A
STRESSFUL WORLD

*A Practical Four-point Strategy
for Replacing Stress with Peace*

RONALD HUTCHCRAFT

THOMAS NELSON PUBLISHERS
Nashville • Camden • New York

Second printing

Published in Nashville, Tennessee, by Thomas Nelson, Inc. and distributed in Canada by Lawson Falle, Ltd., Cambridge, Ontario.

Printed in the United States of America.

Library of Congress Cataloging in Publication Data

Hutchcraft, Ronald.
  Peaceful living in a stressful world.

    1. Christian life—1960-   . 2. Peace of mind. 3.
Stress (Psychology) I. Title.
BV4501.2.H87   1985   248.4   85-10592
ISBN 0-8407-5470-1

Dedication

To my best friend and wife for life, Karen. Your patient and selfless love has created for me an island of sanity in an insane world. "Her husband has full confidence in her and lacks nothing of value" (Prov. 31:10).

Contents

Preface

When a man writes about a subject, he should be highly qualified in that field. That is why I did not write a book about gardening, nuclear physics, or Mozart.

I did write a book about stress. In that area, my credentials are all in order. My life has been a pressure cooker since my sophomore year in high school. I have, for better or worse, learned to walk too fast, talk too fast, and live too fast. In our overheated world, I am not unusual...most everyone I know is trapped in the tentacles of stress.

But who needs another book that just talks about stress? I don't. And I certainly don't have time to write one! Books about stress usually just make us feel more stressful. It was not the stress of my life that gave me something worth writing about...it was *the alternative* I discovered.

Today I am more relaxed, more in control than I have ever been in my adult life. This new peace is not the product of some miracle medication or mystical meditation. And it is certainly not the result of fewer demands on my life—the pressures are greater than they have ever been. That is what makes me so convinced of the strength of this alternative.

In fact, even the process of recording this emotional liberation turned out to be an acid test of its reality. No sooner did I begin writing about stress than the bottom dropped out of my life! Major illnesses, financial crunches, and job crises started detonating like land mines. My bemused conclusion was that when you write about something, it is sure to happen to you. If that is the case, I think I'll write next about "how to handle prosperity." Maybe that will happen, too!

In reality, writing under bombardment became the ultimate laboratory to test the peace I was writing about. And it stood the test.

There is nothing other-worldly or theoretical about this peace. It is active, not passive! Peace has, in fact, cost me something. But not nearly as much as slavery to stress has.

So I have written for people like me—people with responsibility. Parents, executives, leaders, hard workers, students...those are the folks who share my struggle to regain control of lives with accelerators but no brakes.

Because writing a book is one of life's most intense experiences, no one can do it alone. The cover is not big enough to contain the names of all the people who really made this book possible.

My daughter Lisa and my sons Doug and Brad have been my faithful cheerleaders all through the process. Even though it cost them a Daddy for a while, they have been patient and positive. Their youthful wisdom—often expressed in a simple sentence—has instructed me over and over again. And there is nothing like a kiss from one of them to recharge my fading batteries!

With my wife seriously ill during writing time, my sister-in-law Valerie has been the glue that held our personal lives together. Her competence and unselfish serving have made her a heaven-sent "angel of mercy."

My assistant, Esther Malberg, has invested countless hours in preparing the manuscript. I don't know, and I don't think I want to know, how late she worked after hours to meet typing deadlines. Her loyalty and dedication mean a lot.

Bill and Merle Jeanne provided a special place where we could go and begin the book...and Manny and Arlene made available the oasis needed to finish it.

I am grateful to Larry Stone for not letting me rest until I wrote this book and to Peter Gillquist who started as an editor and soon became my soul brother.

There are invisible marks all over this book—they come from my wonderful wife Karen. More than any other person on earth, God has used her to grow and enrich my life. Her love and wisdom are unwritten footnotes on page after page.

In no sense was this book written alone. So many others have coauthored my life and supported this record of what we have learned together.

Many times I would sit back from the typewriter and ask, "Where did *that* come from?" I knew I had written it, but it felt as if Someone else had. As always, He has been my "ever present help," the Resource Center from which all truth comes.

It is, indeed, good advice to "write about what you know about." I have. I have been an expert on real life stress for too long. Then came the showdown described in the pages that follow.

Now I know about something so much better—personal peace under pressure. I want others to have it, too.

Part I
Opening the Door to Peace

1

Living on the Wheel

The showdown began when I stood back and took a painfully honest look at myself. I didn't like what I saw.

The marks of stress were all over me—and the people I love most. Not only did I have the disease myself, I had become a carrier.

Like a certain imported car, I was driven. I had a large, aggressive staff; a sizeable nonprofit budget; a daily and weekly radio broadcast; a high school club in our town; relentless counseling demands; frequent speaking engagements, some weeks, on the average of once a day; overseas assignments; boards and committees... and all the calls and letters that go with this overstuffed schedule.

All this consumed me at a time when my three children needed a Dad, and my wife wanted quality time with the man she had sacrificed so much for.

Everyone's list is different, of course, yet every bit as demanding and potentially destructive. But each of us eventually reaches that same moment of truth I faced: the *showdown with stress*.

The Gerbil Syndrome

The vote was four to one. The issue was whether or not

our family should own a pet.

I lost.

But I did succeed in pushing through some conditions for opening the Hutchcraft Zoo. This pet had to be happy living in a cage and not eat much. That's how a gerbil came to live at our house.

Well, I have to admit, they're cute little fellows. They're just not very smart.

As I sneaked upstairs for a peek at our fuzzy friend, I thought about what gerbil living must be like. I decided to "interview" him.

"Tell me, Gerbie, what do you have planned for today?"

"First," he replied, "breakfast. I'll eat my Gerbil Krispies, and then get started."

"Doing what?"

"Why, the same thing I did yesterday, and the day before that."

"Well, what's that?"

"The wheel."

"The *what*?"

"You heard me, the *wheel*."

Sure enough, he climbed aboard his little wheel and started eagerly running in circles.

After an hour I still found him chugging. "Gerbie," I began gently, "has it ever occurred to you that you're not going anywhere on that wheel? Don't you think you should do something different?"

"You're right," the little guy agreed. "I'm going to make a change." And he did. He went *faster* on the wheel—faster nowhere!

Dumb gerbil! How can he spend his whole life going faster and faster on a wheel to nowhere?

More importantly, how can *we*?

The more I looked at that gerbil that day, the more I realized how much my life was like his! And I knew I was not alone. All of us have our own personal "wheel" that we drive in a barrage of pressures, demands, deadlines, aggravations, and ambitions. We are running hard, burning up a lot of energy—and sometimes burning out.

When my showdown came, I realized I had lost control of large parts of my life. I was, in the words of one stress researcher, "addicted to my own adrenaline."

I actually thought "the wheel" was normal. After all, everyone I knew was spinning as fast as I was. But what's common isn't necessarily normal. If someone lived in a hospital, I guess he could begin to think that being sick was normal. But being surrounded by illness doesn't mean we should be satisfied to be sick. Healthy is normal.

Living on the wheel of stress is *not* how we were meant to live. Even the dictionary hints at that when it tells us that stress is: "a force exerted when one body or body part presses on, pulls on, pushes against, or tends to compress or twist another body or body part."

Those stress verbs fit most of us all too well: "pressed on," "pulled on," "pushed against," "compressed," "twisted." In a word, stress distorts everything—families, friendships, perspective, feelings, physical well-being.

That is why the pharmacist, the counselor, the family doctor all see more of us. We show inside and outside the "stretch marks" of pushing too hard.

Where Have All the Children Gone?

The push begins before many birthdays have passed and keeps pressing right to the end. The absence of peace is in no way a uniquely adult phenomenon.

That something frightening has invaded the innocence of youth can be seen in the titles of recent bestsellers— *The Disappearance of Childhood, The Hurried Child, Our Endangered Children, Children Without Childhood.*

"Carefree" just doesn't describe children as it once did. They are under relentless pressure to perform in everything from Little League to "Aren't they cute?" childhood couples. Since every parent wants his child to be a winner, grades loom very big, very early. And a child may not have even started school when TV introduces him to rape, incest, cohabitation, prostitution, divorce, and nuclear holocaust.

Growing up "stressed out" creates emotionally deformed children. The time bombs start ticking quietly. They will go off later.

As a young man or woman enters junior high then high school, the wheel turns faster. The early stress-shelling becomes a full bombardment.

Teen-agers are under crushing pressure to get grades good enough for college; to decide about virginity before they even understand sex; to buy into the expected party scene where the nicest kids abuse booze, drugs, and each other; and to handle an unprecedented rush of elation, depression, and constant change.

With families pulling apart and the future darkened by a mushroom-shaped cloud, kids are coming apart. According to a recent TV special, in the next thirty minutes

• fifty-seven kids will run away from home;
• twenty-nine children will attempt suicide;
• twenty-two girls under nineteen will have received an abortion to end an unwanted pregnancy;
• fourteen teen-age girls will give birth to illegitimate babies;
• 685 teen-agers—all regular drug users—will take some form of narcotics.

Growing up takes place in a minefield today. Loud, competing voices tell us where to walk—and to walk faster. It's easy to end a life before it has barely begun.

In the years after high school, a young adult may begin to feel like a circus performer who swings from trapeze to trapeze. Each trapeze gets him closer to his final destination. But what about those breathless moments when he's hanging onto nothing—when he's between trapezes!

"Between trapezes" is exactly where many young adults live. They have let go of the old teen-age securities and identities and seek a new adult identity up ahead. Finally on their own, they are barraged with the real-life issues of budgeting, bill paying, choosing a career path, then finding a job in a shrinking market.

If they live at home, no one is quite sure how to act with this intermediate life form. If they go to college, they basically start all over again in almost every area of their lives.

With the life network of family and friends changing, we all are lonely and vulnerable. There's a confusing assortment of people and lifestyles to try on, and it's risky business.

The wheel accelerates as choices and responsibilities grow. Ready or not, the race is on.

Make Your Mark!

No more time to get ready. It's time to produce now! That's society's game plan as we speed through the late twenties and into the thirties. We're in a career niche, for better or worse—for richer, for poorer, too!

We may be faced with the stress of going nowhere in a job—or of going *somewhere*. The more one produces, the more is expected. Whether we wear coveralls, a business suit, or a uniform, there are pressures that "go with the territory." Above us is a ladder to climb. Beneath us are people hungry for our rungs.

When we go home, stress may be waiting there, too. If we go home to singleness, we may face the stress of a situation where *nothing is* really happening. If we go home to a family, we may face the stress of a situation where everything is happening all at once!

Marriage can introduce a joyful sharing and oneness that really completes us as persons. But it also adds a whole new list of pushes and pulls. Now *two* wheels are going at full speed!

Then children join the fun. Babies cry and fall and wet their pants. Then they start to ask questions, choose friends, need rides. Each stage, once looked forward to, now brings even more stressful problems and choices. As children grow, they introduce a whole new schedule to add to our own.

Guess what that makes? More wheels!

All the while, parents mark the unshaped clay of their children's lives, marks that are far more important than any made at work. But work and kids pull on us like two boys yanking on a wishbone. The phone, the doorbell, the bills, the yardwork, the chauffeur service, the doctor, the car, the church—all cause our stress wheels to spin at a dizzying, destructive pace.

We're making marks all right, but look at the marks stress is making on us!

We live in a world that worships beauty, fitness, wealth, and high achievers. As we move through our forties and fifties, those may slip away, totally out of reach.

A new identity search makes change look very tempting—a change of job, location, church, image, lifestyle, marriage partner. A woman with more daytime hours on her hands sets out to find herself in a career; a man struggles with the temptation to "prove himself" with a sexual conquest outside his marriage; a couple faces reality when the empty nest reveals an empty marriage.

Midlife was built to be that time when a man or woman enjoys the harvest of seeds sown throughout a lifetime. That harvest should include being sought for counsel, enjoying grandchildren, feeling free to enjoy their partners exclusively, knowing enough security to help a hurting world.

But our pressurized world is not always so kind. The harvest of midlife is sometimes bitter fruit.

Shuffleboard, senility, and Social Security—that's the youth cult image of the senior years. Because little in life prepares us for the unique stresses of later life, it can be a time of Social *In*security! We have been children, teen-agers, young adults, growing "mark makers," midlifers. We can, if we try, understand their stresses. But they have never run the wheel at our age, and they can't understand ours.

Retirement poses one of life's major challenges, one from which some folks never recover. After all these years of being identified by work, who are we without those jobs? Questions about our value are compounded by the feeling we are being left out more and more by younger people we love.

We sense that we have forever left the "Pepsi Generation" for the "Geritol Generation." Our bodies start to let us down. It won't do all the things it used to, and it doesn't always keep up with our minds and our dreams.

The most devastating stress in life, the researchers tell us, is the loss of our spouses. That is most likely to happen in those senior years. Our sense of loneliness and mortality grows as old friends leave us, too.

These later years are happy for some, but hard years for almost all. There is no graduation from stress. It follows us through the years, wearing a different face as we grow.

And true to its definition, it is twisting and deforming us and those we love every step of the way.

The "As-Soon-As" Syndrome

It was summer vacation on Cape Cod, and I had a wife and three kids "psyched" for one of Daddy's great adventures. We were going to climb a giant sand dune and find the ocean. The sign said the ocean was beyond the dune—or, as it turned out, the dunes.

The first mountain of sand was fun; the second, less fun; the third, no fun at all. Every time we reached the top of a dune, all we found was another dune!

Three short pairs of legs wanted out. Like Balboa, pressing to discover the Pacific, I would not be deterred. As we started up each new hill, I assured my troops that the ocean was just over the top. I've never again been wrong so many times in one afternoon in my life. Yes, we did finally stumble over one last sand dune into the ocean. But by that time my proud expedition had turned into the march of the zombies!

I was afflicted that day by a form of wishful thinking called the "as-soon-as" syndrome. The hard part will be over, as soon as we get to the top of this particular peak. Unfortunately, there is always another mountain.

I kept postponing my showdown with stress, innocently

believing that my life would slow down when the current crisis passed. It never happened.

We "gerbils" cling to the false hope that the spin will slow down "*as soon as*" we...

Get into high school
Get out of high school
Get a car
Get more friends
Get a job
Get a raise
Get a mate
Get a house
Get a bigger house
Get finished with this project
Get children
Get this weight off
Get well
Get a vacation
Get my pension
Get something to do now that we're retired

I am convinced that every "as soon as" opens the door to another. The wheel of stress runs full speed from the cradle to the grave. It is a fact of life.

When it comes to surgery, I've gotten off pretty easy—only one operation in my whole life. The surgeon did his carving, and I didn't feel a thing—for a while. The anesthetic masked the pain, but it soon wore off. Reality set in. And the scar will be there for the rest of my life.

Eventually the pain of stress becomes unbearable, too. But instead of finding a solution, we usually settle for sedation! There is temporary relief that feels like a solution—until the anesthetic wears off. Then we have to live with greater pain and deeper scars.

We escape with an airplane ticket or a tennis racquet or a TV set. Alcohol, medication, music, or sleep can mask the pain. We can hide the fire at home in a never-home schedule, and people will even praise us for our dedication. We can take our unmet needs into a new career where we will use and be used. We can chase pleasure, only to find that the harder we chase it, the faster it runs.

The Showdown with Stress

Cape Hatteras is a windblown barrier reef on the coast of North Carolina. It must be the storm center of the East Coast. In winter, the blizzards seldom miss there; in summer, the hurricanes are frequent visitors.

When I visited there recently, I tried to imagine those Outer Banks in a hurricane. Imagining was enough for me! It seemed to me that the greatest destruction would come from the battering winds on the Atlantic side. A local veteran corrected me. Surprisingly, the worst of the storm comes from the sheltered back side of the Cape—from the bay.

The reason? The hurricane gales drive walls of water across the Cape and into the bay. Then the force of the wind holds the water back. That is, until the hurricane subsides. Then, when there is no longer anything holding back the water that has built up, the deadly flood hits the Cape, all from the buildup during the storm!

Pounded for years by rushing and responsibility, I have felt like a human version of Cape Hatteras. Each successive storm was taking its toll and creating a bigger buildup. I had been holding back the flood waters for years, but I was worn down and weakening. I had seen the health, the family, the happiness of too many people washed away by the ravages of stress.

I wanted desperately to get control of my life again before that happened. I realized that I could not *outgrow* stress. It has chased me through every stage of life. I decided I could not *outlast* stress—there would always be another mountain just beyond the one I was climbing now. And I found I could not *outrun* stress, but only postpone the inevitable day of reckoning with its toll.

There had to be a way off the wheel, an alternative to my

tyranny of stress. Sitting on the lakeside porch of a mountain cabin, I reached a "no turning back" conclusion. I said aloud, "I must have something better."

2

Peace Is Not Passive

I knew what the something better was—peace. It had been a part of my Christian beliefs for years. I had, in fact, preached peace. But I was practicing pressure.

I never really understood peace. I kept waiting for it, praying for it to fall on my swirling life like a soft blanket of heavenly dew. It never did. Oh, there were occasional tastes of it—a quiet vacation spot, a spiritual mountaintop, a good day. But, like dew, it always seemed to evaporate in the heat of traffic jams and people jams in real life.

Peace has often seemed like a warm, fuzzy word that somehow didn't settle my "drivenness." It had a cotton candy quality to it—pretty to look at, sweet to taste, but nothing really there to sink your teeth into.

Yet, a peaceful person was, more than ever, what I wanted to be. If there was a cure for the cancer of stress, it had to be peace.

And then, in a challenge written centuries ago, I began to discover the pathway to personal peace. I had been looking for a way to *let* peace happen to me. Instead I found a way to *make* it happen with God's help.

For all of us trapped on the wheel, it is, indeed, "something better."

The Eye of the Storm

Peace, though, is not an escape from the turbulence around us.

I will never forget the day Hurricane Belle met us for our vacation on Long Island. She hit us with hundred-mile-an-hour winds, leaving a tragic trail of destruction across the area. The five of us were huddled together in the living room of our lodge, listening to the ravaging winds around us.

And then it stopped. The sudden calm was almost startling. There was the most beautiful sense of peace. But the storm wasn't finished. Belle returned with another frightening blast.

We experienced that night something I had only read about before—the eye of the hurricane. In the middle of every savage hurricane is that eye, where it is perfectly still.

The peace alternative that is calming my life doesn't offer a world without storms. In fact, some of my own storms have even intensified. But it is possible to live at peace in the eye of the storm!

Let It Begin with Me

If "all's well that ends well," then our son's fifth-grade concert was a success. These kids were leaving elementary school, and that concert is the closest thing they have to a graduation. Now my son Doug was not exactly a member of the Philharmonic or the Vienna Boys' Choir, but I wouldn't miss his performance for anything!

Oh, they had their share of squeaky reeds, imaginative harmonies, and giggles. But they made up for all the "muffs" (that's what Doug calls them) with their grand finale. Like an angel choir, they sang in perfect unison: "Let there be peace on earth and let it begin with me."

It was tissue time. Maybe it was those innocent faces, or our adult awareness of what a violent place their world really is. But they sang the truth. If there is to be peace on earth, or in my family or my office or my friends, then it must begin with me. But how does peace begin?

Peace is an intensely individual issue. The only hope of finding peace in my environment is finding *personal* peace.

And it is there to be found. I know that because of the last will and testament of Jesus Christ. It is the promise He made just before He died and rose again: "Peace I leave with you; *my peace I give you.* I do not give to you as the world gives. Do not let your hearts be troubled and do not be afraid" (John 14:27).

I'm glad to hear that Jesus' peace isn't like any peace the world gives. His is uninterrupted, not occasional. It takes us safely through the storms, not like our "run from it" sedatives.

I know this peace works when every other human glue comes unstuck. I've seen it in a young mother, cradling her children by the steel gray casket of her husband; in men out of work for months; in the face of a devastated terminal cancer patient; in a young couple as they bury the five-year-old daughter finally claimed by leukemia.

And I have experienced this peace intermittently—through the loss of our first baby, the helplessness of having no more food and no more money, the trauma of a near-fatal accident, the lingering death of my dad, the crush of twenty years of people's lives in my care.

This is powerful peace! But it is not ours automatically. You can live your whole life without consistently knowing this peace.

"No Rest for the Wicked"

Last night we were hit by an Atlantic storm that certainly got our attention! This morning I walked down to the beach at high tide. The ocean didn't seem very friendly. She was heaving angrily, erupting into thundering whitecaps. Great walls of water were forming, one atop another, as far as my eyes could see. The ocean was dark, seething, troubled. There in front of me was, according to the Bible, a dramatic picture of a heart without God's peace:

The wicked are like the tossing sea, which cannot rest, whose waves cast up mire and mud. "There is no peace," says my God, "for the wicked" (Isa. 57:20-21).

"Cannot rest... no peace." That's just like the sea—incurably restless. And maybe that describes your inner turmoil. Nothing seems big enough to fill the hole in our hearts. Every relationship, every achievement, every experience has been a disappointment—nothing has been able to satisfy that incurable restlessness! God said, "There is no peace for the wicked."

Our first reaction is to say, "I know some of those wicked people He's talking about. I'm sure glad I'm not one of them." The wicked are mentioned again in the New Testament: "The way of peace they do not know" (Rom. 3:17).

Who *are* these people who don't know peace? The verses around that passage tell us. "There is no one righteous, not even one;... no one who seeks God. All have turned away... no one will be declared righteous in His sight by observing the law... all have sinned and fall short of the glory of God" (Rom. 3:10-12; 20, 23).

We look for loopholes, but there are too many "no ones" and "alls" here to ignore. In God's eyes, you and I have a deadly sin problem that makes peace impossible. Our own hearts tell us that we're included. The storms rage about us—and inside us—with an occasional slackening, but no real peace.

The sun came out today after last night's chilling storm. Everything seems warmer, more alive. It is, of course, that blazing star that creates our seasons, provides our warmth, lights our darkness, and gives us life. But what if the earth should suddenly be shifted from its precise orientation around the sun? All life on earth would be affected. Death would be the result.

Our "me-firstness" called sin has driven us out of our Son-orbit. We were created to revolve around the God who made us. But we have gone off on our own. And it is that meandering that is robbing us of the warmth, the color, the light, the life we were created to experience. Without spiritual realignment—which brings us back into orbit—all ordered life will cease.

The Peace Place

Without God then, we are terribly alone in a turbulent world. We were made for His companionship—we have no peace because we aren't at peace with Him! But we can be, not because we deserve it, but because He loves us. The ancient Jewish prophet totaled the price for our peace:

The *punishment* that *brought us peace* was upon Him (Isa. 53:5).

The "Him" is Jesus Christ, the One who said, "My peace I give you." That's why He can offer peace. He purchased it with His life. His death paid for all the sins of all the days of my life, and the treaty between God and me is signed in His blood! In the words of the Bible, "Since we have been justified [made right with God] through faith, we have peace with God through our Lord Jesus Christ" (Rom. 5:1).

Who are the "we" who are finally at peace with God? How can we be part of them? We have to visit the Peace Place. If we judge just by looking, we will not think it is the place to look for peace. But it's the only place we'll ever find it. "Making peace through His blood, shed on the cross" (Col. 1:20).

Peace begins at the cross where Jesus died. Our sins are erased when we make our way to that cross and say, "Jesus, I believe that what You've done here is for me—for my sins. You bought me. You've got me. Take me, I'm Yours!"

At that moment we have the most beautiful sense of finally coming home. Because we have stepped into peace *with* God, we have access from now on to peace *from* God—the end of a lifelong search for peace to "begin in me!"

I remember when it began for Joanne. She and her husband came to my office for a counseling session. They had already given up any hope of saving their marriage. They just wanted to figure out how to announce their divorce to their twelve-year-old son.

The air was charged as I asked Joanne and Mark to fight *for* those eighteen years instead of fighting *over* them. Joanne had stored up years of hurt from Dave's preoccupation with his work and his failure to lead their home. Now, the tensions of no job and no paycheck had brought the pot to a boil.

Joanne talked at a machine-gun clip, spitting out a heart full of anxieties. Afraid to try and afraid to give up, she was strung as tightly as a violin. She interspersed her verbal barrages with welling tears.

Joanne and Mark didn't get that divorce. In their despair, they were willing to accept my proposal of a visit to the Peace Place.

"But we're active in our church," they had first protested. "We're leaders! Religion hasn't helped us."

"I'm not surprised," I said. "Religion can't give you the new love you need, the grace to forgive. You need a relationship with Jesus Christ Himself."

That afternoon Joanne and Mark gave all the broken pieces of their lives to Jesus Christ. He left my office determined. She left amazingly at peace. Their subsequent weekends away built foundations for new ways of getting along. And Joanne was finally relaxed enough to give Mark a chance.

It was Joanne's next-door neighbor who was most intrigued by the changes she saw in her ever-hyper friend. Finally, the neighbor could contain her curiosity no longer. She blurted out, "What are you taking, Joanne? In all these years I've never seen you like this. You're...you're calm!"

That inner rest can belong to anyone who belongs to Jesus Christ. Like a little child nestled in his Daddy's arms, he has found a safe place.

Safety explains that large structure at the entrance to the harbor in Stamford, Connecticut. Our dear friends sail out of that harbor...and once in a while they take some "land-lubbers" along.

I asked my nautical friend what all that mechanized equipment was as we motored into the harbor. He told me that it was the hurricane gate.

He must have seen the questions in my eyes. "When a heavy storm is moving up the coast," he explained, "they activate this gate. It's strong enough to withstand anything that's blown against it so far. So once you're behind that hurricane gate, you're protected from the worst of the storm. You may get blown around...but you *won't sink*."

Isn't that exactly what we stress-tossed people need—a safe place? We weren't built to battle the full force of the world. Jesus Christ is, for all who know Him, that safe place. Sure, we will still get knocked around—violently, at times. But we won't be defeated.

How Come It Isn't Working?

I'd known Christ for a long time. I had, as I said earlier, spoken publicly about the Prince of Peace for nearly twenty-five years. I had watched Him bring a "Peace, be still" to the storms in thousands of lives.

How then did my life get so out of control?

I was intrigued by the soul-baring testimony of a veteran pastor at a recent conference. For over twenty years his parish has been the inner city. He admitted to all that he had been on the edge of night called burnout. He had expended so much in his ministry that he had nothing left to give. Some friends suggested a counselor to him, one who had helped other ministers through the crisis of burnout. The first assignment he received from the counselor was unusual: "Go find a quiet place for a day, and just draw pictures that represent your life right now."

He returned a week later with his masterpieces. As soon as he described the first one to the conference participants, I felt as if an arrow had been shot into my heart. I could have been speaking his words: "This is my car, driving along my street. But I'm not in the front seat where I belong. I'm in the back seat, and there are nine people in the front seat, all fighting over the steering wheel. I have totally lost control of my own schedule, my priorities—my life!''

Oh, I knew my relationship with God was secure—not because of how I was holding onto Him, but because of how *He* was holding onto me! Peace was my personal legacy as a child of God, but stress was calling the shots. And that's how my search to regain control of "the steering wheel" began.

After years of thinking of peace in passive terms, I was in for a liberating surprise.

I knew if there was real substance to peace, I'd find out about it in the Bible. Using a concordance, I began to study—not just read—every verse that dealt with peace, rest, quietness, anything that might help me understand.

It was a simple verse that finally grabbed my soul and wouldn't let go. It hasn't let go since. For me, it held the very key to peace. David wrote in Psalm 34:14:

Seek peace and pursue it.

Seek peace? *Pursue* it? Wait a minute! Those are *action* words! David was saying that *peace is not passive.*

But David did not live in this twentieth-century vise! What did he know about stress? After all, he was a Jewish king, living in comfort and luxury.

Not when he wrote the thirty-fourth Psalm, he wasn't! David was a fugitive, running for his life. King Saul, the first king of Israel, was "losing his grip," as they say. His jealousy over David's popularity and his fears of losing his throne had almost driven him mad. David was not only on the Most Wanted List, he *was* the Most Wanted List! His days were filled with running and battling starvation. His nights were filled with the fear of not living to see morning. Stress was breathing down his neck every minute of every day.

David was being pursued when he wrote that eye-opening spiritual secret, "Seek peace and pursue it."

But a life can't be rebuilt on one isolated verse, as appealing as it may sound. Is this pursuit of peace a significant theme elsewhere in God's Word?

Peace Under Pressure

We hear the word *refugee* a lot on the evening news broadcast these days—Palestinian, Southeast Asian, Haitian. A turbulent world drives people from their lifelong homes almost daily.

When the apostle Peter wrote his first letter, it was addressed to refugees: "God's elect, strangers in the world, scattered throughout Pontus, Galatia, Cappadocia, Asia and Bithynia" (1 Pet. 1:1). They had been driven from their homes in Jerusalem because they had dared to take a stand for Jesus Christ. Many of them had, no doubt, left behind the freshly dug graves of loved ones who had died in anti-Christian violence.

It is little wonder that Peter's theme is one of suffering. He wrote about how to live when persecuted, pressured, and pursued. His challenge to these superstressed saints reached back into the Old Testament. The words are familiar:

"Whoever would love life and see good days...He must *seek peace and pursue it*" (1 Pet. 3:10-11).

There it was again!

Then there was Jeremiah, who, like Peter, ministered to uprooted people. God had been trying to get through to the Jewish people for a long time, but their spiritual receiver was off the hook! After ignoring countless prophetic warnings to come home to Him, the guillotine of discipline finally fell. The conquering Babylonian army carried back to their country most of the people of Israel.

In a sense, the Jews were now prisoners in another culture. God's timetable would keep them there in Babylon for seventy years. The natural response would be to pout, drag their feet, make no contribution. But Jeremiah has surprising advice for folks who feel trapped in a depressing situation: "*Seek the peace* and prosperity of the city to which I have carried you into exile" (Jer. 29:7).

They will be sustained if they seek God's peace! Again, it's something you look for and track down!

Writing letters is one of the least enjoyable parts of my job, and usually one of the last tasks to get done. If the apostle Paul had been a procrastinating letter writer like me, half the New Testament might be missing! Fortunately, Paul was a more faithful correspondent, authoring thirteen books of the New Testament—even though he had to be put in prison sometimes to catch up on his writing!

In at least four of his letters, Paul urged readers to go on this active quest for peace in their everyday lives. The thought is the same, but the settings are different. The people he touched with this peace pursuit are easy to identify with; their stresses have a modern ring to them.

Because Timothy was a young man, he needed some directive advice to complement Paul's challenges to minister. In his second letter to Timothy, Paul talked about personal purity, keeping the body special.

First, he urges him to "Flee the evil desires of youth" (2 Tim. 2:22). That's the negative. Too many times we only tell our kids what they should *not* do. Get rid of that music, those friends, that amusement! But nature abhors a vacuum. Jesus said you cannot leave unoccupied a house (a man) that has just had an evil spirit evicted. If you do, that evil spirit will come back "with...seven other spirits more wicked than itself" (Matt. 12:45). If you're going to prohibit something, then you need to *pursue* something else.

That's how Paul advised Timothy to combat living by his youthful glands. "Flee the evil desires of youth, *and pursue* righteousness, faith, love and *peace* (2 Tim. 2:22).

He took away one vice—lust—and gave him four virtues! Part of the prescription for being young and living pure is to pursue *peace*!

The second call from Paul to be a "peace activist" was to the church at Rome. There the Christians came in as many flavors as ice cream. Rome was, of course, the crossroads of the Empire. People from all walks of life were finding Christ in that city—the slaves, the slave owners, the proudly religious Jews, the proficiently pagan Gentiles, the rich patrician, the blue-collar plebeian.

When those folks got together for church, there was a lot of potential for fireworks—the kind that rip churches apart. This church was not a melting pot. It was a *stew* where the beef remains beef, the potatoes are all potato, and the carrots have no plans to become onions.

Paul's letter indicates that the pot was sometimes boiling. The issue was vast differences in lifestyle. They agreed on the basics of knowing Christ, but they disagreed on everything from Christian food to who should celebrate what sacred day. Like Christians today, they had a way of emphasizing the *10* percent that separated them instead of the *90* percent that united them!

Paul stepped into this turmoil as the spiritual referee, and he refused merely to take sides. Instead, he talked about their energy and where it should be expended: "Let us therefore *make every effort to do what leads to peace*" (Rom. 14:19).

Apparently, the folks at Ephesus needed that counsel, too. They needed unity, not so much because of divisions within them, but because of paganism all around them. One historian described Ephesus as the "moral zoo of the Roman world." It was the center of the worship of Diana, a religion that made the prostitutes into priests! The church at Ephesus was founded in fire, a bonfire that was used to burn a mountain of relics from Satanic, occult practices (see Acts 19:18-20).

These were believers living in defiling pagan pressures all day long, a lot like we are. Their margin of survival was to stick together. So Paul wrote, *"Make every effort* to keep the unity of the Spirit through *the bond of peace"* (Eph. 4:3).

Peace takes hard work—pursuit!

A fourth call to peaceful living came to the busy, busy church at Thessalonica. Paul said they were a church which was running full speed in an "evangelism explosion."

These were dynamite believers, but ones who could blow up their own lives in the midst of serving the Lord. Paul praised their witness, expressed fatherly pride in his "children," then gave them this simple preventive maintenance counsel: "Make it *your ambition* to lead *a quiet life*, to mind your own business and to work with your hands...so that your daily life may win the respect of outsiders" (1 Thess. 4:11). Paul said to push for a sane lifestyle.

Whether it's the stresses of youthful temptation, or friction between different people, or the pull of a pagan environment, or a life busy with Christian service, the challenge is the same: *pursue, work for, push for peace*. Certainly to the apostle Paul, peace was not passive!

Heroes—that's what people are who take a stand against the spiral of stress! George did. His company really liked him. That was evidenced by the growing collection of awards on his den wall. They liked him so much that they offered him a much better position with a much better paycheck—halfway across the country! Because of management policy, it was possible he could get a demotion if he refused this promotion.

George knew his family needed to stay where they were. Their church, their school, their friends, their securities were all involved. And he knew that with more money and prestige would come a lot more pressure. There before him was the ladder to success and the push to climb it—and the threat of falling off if he didn't climb.

But George and his family took their stand. With courage and conviction, they sought peace. They said no. He didn't get demoted, by the way, and he's still collecting those company awards. And that priceless root system in his family is still thriving and growing!

The pursuit of peace demands active choices such as that. They are choices founded on a symphony of scriptural challenges. Jesus told us, "Blessed are the *peacemakers*, for they will be called the children of God" (Matt. 5:9).

Peace doesn't just happen. It is made, built, constructed by the immediate members of God's family. James described the process of going after peace in farming terms, "Peace-makers who *sow in peace* raise *a harvest of righteousness*" (James 3:18).

Our family loves to visit Pennsylvania Dutch country, the home of the unchanged Amish. Farming is their life—old-fashioned farming with nonmotorized machinery like mules and hands. We have watched them sow their crops, and it is not a passive process. It is nonstop, back-breaking effort from sunrise to sunset. They think it's worth it for the glori-ous harvest it produces. Peace is like that, according to James. Working hard to cultivate it results in a barnful of good things!

The writer of Hebrews joins the Peace Chorus when he describes "a Sabbath-rest for the people of God" (Heb. 4:9). He urges us to

Make every effort to enter that rest (Heb. 4:11).

One of the great sleep-inducers in school was learning the "parts of speech." Sleep teaching must be effective because I still remember some of them. There are active and passive verbs, right? Well, I would like to create an exciting new ad-dition to the English language. It's called the "active noun." After pursuing it through the Bible, what else can we call peace? It is a bold, aggressive, "go for it" active noun!

Saints as diverse as David and Peter and Paul told us to go looking for peace. And certainly they were men who knew something about pursuit! David had, no doubt, gone looking for many a wandering sheep. If a shepherd waits for a delin-quent lamb to come home by himself, he'll be minus one lamb. Sheep don't come to the shepherd—he has to go after them! That veteran sheep-seeker was the one who told us to go after peace the same way.

Peter's pursuits were to be found underwater. No bass, no

bucks. Can we imagine a veteran fisherman like Peter just sitting on the beach next to a bucketful of worms, waiting for some friendly fish to check in? The professional angler becomes an expert on the bait, the currents, the weather, the water, the fish. A fisherman is a pursuer—just like Peter said a "peace candidate" has to be.

Pursuing Christians was Paul's pre-conversion specialty. As Saul of Tarsus, he was the number-one hit man for the Jerusalem Mafia. When he couldn't find enough Christians in Jerusalem, he pursued them to Damascus. Well, almost. Jesus intercepted him on the way. Paul knew what it was to chase down a target with stubborn determination, and he told us to chase peace the same way.

The more I investigated it, the more convinced I became. David's original challenge *is* the path to personal peace: "Seek peace, and pursue it" (Ps. 34:14). That's the beacon that penetrates the stormy darkness of our stress-filled night, and gives us a way to find home!

The Peace Plan

The Vietnam conflict had divided America for nearly a decade. Richard Nixon was running for President. He captured the attention of the American voters with what he called, "a secret plan for peace." In my opinion, if you have a plan for peace, it shouldn't be a secret—especially if it's for *personal* peace.

I am learning that no matter how turbulent, how painful, my life may seem right now, peace is there for the pursuing! If I wait for it, it won't come. *If I go after it, I'll find it.*

Gaining personal peace requires a commitment and a plan. The commitment is to dethrone stress as ruler, and to do whatever is necessary to enthrone peace. Strong corrective action must be taken to regain control, clear decisions made, courageous stands taken. You have to reach that point where the pain of staying the same has become greater than the pain of changing.

That initial commitment, in itself, won't do it. A peace

plan that will give peace a chance to take hold is needed. And, as the Bible showed me so clearly, the plan is no secret.

If we are ready for a commitment to *pursue peace* aggressively and consistently, then we're ready to explore the four-point plan for peace. It is the plan I came upon from the Holy Scriptures in my own pursuit of peace.

1. Protect the quiet centers.
2. Remove the roots of restlessness.
3. Attack the stress centers.
4. Build peaceful habits.

Like hunting buried treasure, the pursuit of peace is an adventure. If you're tired of the poverty of rat-race living, then you're ready for the adventure.

Stress has been driving too long, in your family, your work, and your faith. Your sanity has been twisted and deformed long enough. Peaceful is how we were meant to live. It's *normal*!

Inside us, around us are cries for something better. God has given us the map that leads to the treasure. It begins at the cross where our peace was bought and paid for, and it leads us to that "eye of the storm" where we "let the peace of Christ rule in [our] hearts" (Col. 3:15).

Part II
Protecting the Five Quiet Centers

3

Practicing His Presence

Our town must be the flood capital of northern New Jersey. Three rivers converge there, setting the stage for a spring emergency almost every year. Realtors joke that houses near the river come complete with a rowboat!

A few weeks ago our area was hit with the flood of the century. Five inches of rain melted ten inches of snow, and all that pressure caused two dams to break. The deluge hit so fast that people had only minutes to evacuate.

The devastation was tragic. We drove into the worst of the flood area to check on some friends' houses and to offer our help. I will never forget the sight of that river on the rampage. The water was boiling, churning, ripping away anyone and anything in its path. We watched what had been a living room or a garage swept downstream like a matchbox. The force of the flood carried away automobiles, furniture, houses, animals. It seemed that nothing could resist the rush of the river.

Nothing, that is, except the trees. The floods came and went, but those giant oaks right on the riverbank stood unmoved. They have something that houses and cars don't have—*roots*! A tree is held in place by a sprawling root system that even the flood of the century cannot move!

The "floods" that tear most at us don't usually come from

the river. We feel the force of lives flooded with demands, deadlines, decisions, deficits, and disappointments. If the "heavy rains" were not enough, we get hit with the deluge from a dam that breaks—the accident, the illness, the injury, the betrayal, the loss, the family crisis. Some of us feel dangerously close to being swept downstream.

All of us "flood victims" urgently need the lesson of the riverside oaks: *If you don't want to get carried away, take care of your roots!*

We can't stop the flood, but we can develop a root system that provides a steady supply of peace and poise and calm. Once roots are put down, they must be protected as fiercely as a mother lion guards her cubs.

The Roots of Peace

We don't have peace because we don't go after it. That's the Bible's simple assessment. Peace will not come after us. Only stress does that.

When the Bible tells us "*seek* peace and *pursue* it" (Ps. 34:14), those verbs are full of intensity. *Pursue* is the Greek word *dioko*, the "go for it!" verb of the Bible. It means to run after, strive for, press hard.

In one place, *dioko* alludes to an Olympic track star who will "*press on* toward the goal to win the prize" (Phil. 3:14). He surges toward the finish line, veins bulging, muscles straining, lungs exploding. He is giving 110 percent to get the gold! If our trophy is a sane personal lifestyle, we have to press for it with everything we've got!

The "go for it" verb in Hebrew is used to describe a "*hunted* antelope" (Isa. 13:14). "I'm bringing home some game tonight," the backwoodsman announces as he disappears out the cabin door. With cunning determination he stalks his prey until he brings it in. If personal peace is what we're hunting, we have to go after it with the relentless determination of the hunter.

Folks with a drinking problem even get into the act when the Bible talks about pursuit. "Woe to those who rise early in the morning/to run after their drinks" (Isa. 5:11). They're hooked—they *must* have a drink, and they will look until they find one. In much the same way, a life under control belongs only to those who are addicted enough to demand it.

This aggressive, all-out pursuit of peace begins at the roots. The roots of peace can best be described as *"quiet centers."* They are five stabilizing nonnegotiables that hold us in place.

To be sure, there are plenty of stress centers in life, too. We will attack them later. But peace originates in the quiet centers of life.

Stress centers make lots of noise. They demand attention and tend to take over. Quiet centers are, well, quiet. They are usually neglected, often pushed aside, frequently thrown overboard. But there is no peace without them.

Remember, the pursuit of peace is a go-for-it crusade. The first aggressive step is to establish five quiet centers, then to guard them tenaciously against any intrusion. They form a personal root system that can resist any flood.

The Pressure and the Presence

In April 1963 the nuclear submarine *Thresher* vanished about two hundred miles off the coast of New England. It had been undergoing deep submergence tests when radio contact was lost. Frantic attempts to contact, then to locate, the crew, were in vain.

Apparently, the *Thresher* had gone deeper than it was pressurized to go. In one terrifying moment, the pressure on the outside simply became greater than the pressure on the inside. The ocean came in like jets of steam, and 129 American sailors were lost.

Unequalized pressure causes people to collapse, too. The first of the five quiet centers provides a Presence greater than the pressure of the day ahead.

We're built to begin our day with our Creator. It started with Adam who met "the LORD God as He was walking in the garden in the cool of the day" (Gen. 3:8). Since then, men and women have been incomplete—whether they recognize it or not—without their morning walk with God.

David told us while literally running for his life, "Seek peace and pursue it." With stress his constant pursuer, how could he be so preoccupied with peace? He explained: "I sought the LORD, and he answered me;/he delivered me from all my fears./Those who look to him are radiant;/...Taste and see that the LORD is good" (Ps. 34:4-5, 8).

David could then go on to "pursue peace" because he had found his quiet center. It came from his time with the Lord!

Even Jesus protected that quiet center. The Gospels show us that He was up early every morning. When those twelve disciples first started following Jesus, they must have wondered why He was never there when they woke up! His absence is explained in this way: "Jesus often withdrew to lonely places and prayed" (Luke 5:16). Each day seemed to bring a new crisis for Him, not unlike our days. Luke records it this way:

The Crisis	His Quiet Center	The Result
Being surrounded by people who needed His help	He prayed (see Luke 5:16)	New mercy to give
Sorting out time priorities	He prayed (see Luke 4:42)	Knew what He had to do
Making a major life decision	He prayed (see Luke 6:12)	Clearcut choices
Needing more resources than were available	He prayed (see Luke 9:16)	Miraculous supply
Facing pain and suffering	He prayed (see Luke 9:28)	Courage

Sometimes, in our living room visitors see this strange creature sitting in the recliner. It appears to be a newspaper with legs. Actually, it's only me, cheering myself up with news of today's strikes, wars, and homicides.

That is often the scene when my daughter suddenly appears on my lap (so much for the evening news). She will wrap an arm or two around me and announce brightly, "Daddy, it's cuddle time!" And then it happens—Dad melts all over the easy chair.

"Cuddle time" is special in any relationship. Relationship with God is no exception. To "keep your cool" throughout today's pressures, cuddle time with the Lord is not optional.

If it's not considered a must, there will be an almost endless list of reasons it can't be done...

"By the time I get everybody off in the morning and the house put back together, there's no time left!"

"There's barely time to make it to *work*!"

"Are you kidding? Do you know what time I have to leave for school?"

"My heart doesn't even start until ten-thirty!"

In essence, all the excuses inadvertently say the same thing: "Sorry, Lord. I just can't squeeze You in." As a result, we race into another day spiritually and emotionally "unzipped."

The harder it is to find time with the Lord, the more one needs that time with the Lord. Martin Luther said, "If I'm going to have a busy day, I spend an hour with the Lord. If I'm going to have a *very* busy day, I spend *two* hours." I have a long way to go before I can say that, but I can catch that spirit. My stress-saturated days leave me no choice but fighting for that quiet center with the Lord! It is absolutely crucial to the pursuit of peace.

Five Action Steps

There is no better way to start the day with our "act together" than to touch base with the Lord. The commitment to an uncompromised time with Him involves five action steps.

First, *set a spot*.

Without a definite time and place, this quiet center will be crowded right out. The Lord Jesus needs to be part of our morning schedule. Most of us have our morning repairs down to a predictable block of time. If we want to spend fifteen minutes with Jesus, those minutes have to show up on the alarm clock setting the night before. We must set aside a consistent meeting place, too, where our Bible, notebook, and prayer list are waiting for us.

Second, *clear your mind*.

God wants to transmit to us during that time together. We can't get the message if there's too much interference on the line. With the demands of the day already happening in our minds, it's hard to find room for the voice of the Lord. Yet God tells us to "be still, and know that I am God" (Ps. 46:10).

Settle down for a few minutes and ask Him to help you focus on Him. Consciously resist the "static" of interruptions and distractions. Protecting this quiet center involves more than just guarding the time and place. The intimacy of that time must be guarded by concentrating on the Person you are with.

I'm sure cuddle time would not mean much to my children if I kept reading the newspaper in the middle of their hugs. The rest of the day can't be allowed to fill up our Jesus-time. Instead, let His time fill up the rest of the day.

Thirdly, *open your hands*.

You have accumulated a new handful since yesterday morning: a gift to thank someone for, a wound from someone close, a person you are deeply concerned for, a part of you that's being kept from Him, a heavy schedule, an unanswered question, a preoccupying worry. Cuddle time is time to turn all that over to the Prince of Peace.

The fourth step is to *get an assignment*.

God always has a word for today, and it is communicated through the only book He ever wrote, the Bible. Like pursuing peace, reading the Bible was never meant to be a passive experience. It is not merely meeting with a book—but with a *Person*. We are looking for something to *do* today, not just something to *know*. We respond by staying with His words until they can be applied to something we will face that day. That's how we discover our assignment!

Recording the dialogue in a spiritual diary places us on the receiving end of that beautiful promise:

Great peace have they who love your law, and *nothing can make them stumble* (Ps. 119:165).

Fifth, after we set our spot, clear our mind, open our hands, and get our assignment, we set our course.

Think through the events and people that will be filling your day. Pray through each of them in advance. Consciously turn over to Christ the specific anticipations of this twenty-four hours. As you do, be attentive to any instructions or ideas He plants in your heart about those "turnovers."

It may have only been a few minutes, but I find myself walking away from that cuddle time with a deep-down sense of well-being...peace, if you will.

Time with the Lord is a well from which to draw all day long. That well has to be guarded vigilantly to protect it from pollution or neglect.

When that Jesus-time is the number-one priority of your schedule, your soul is anchored in the harbor only He can provide. Don't compromise His time for anything or anyone!

Staying in Touch

My friend Bill was in his last day of a grueling two-week training program called Wilderness School. He and his fellow "pioneers" had conquered the challenges of rock climbing, solo survival overnights, climbing, hiking, and demanding tests of physical endurance. It was time to return to base camp, and his leader gave Bill two choices: he could ride back with the leader or run those last ten miles. Bill chose to run.

The first mile was almost enough to paralyze his exhausted body. At the point of giving out, he caught up with a buddy who was running, too. Still pushing along the trail, they shared their feelings, their determination, and a few laughs. Much to his body's surprise, Bill ran the entire ten miles and surged into base camp on an exhilarated wave of adrenaline.

As he replayed that run in his mind, Bill told us what made the difference. "I ran much farther than I thought I could because *someone I cared about was running with me.*"

A typical day in my life seems like a long-distance marathon, and I'm already tired from the mountain I climbed yesterday! The hours ahead are filled. Since I began my active pursuit of peace, I am learning what a difference His presence makes in my personal marathon. Jesus promised, "Surely I will be with you always, to the very end of the age" (Matt. 28:20).

My daily race will be as lonely and overwhelming as ever if I am not consciously aware of His peace-giving Presence.

I've been meeting the Lord in the morning for a long time. The regular entries in my spiritual diary recall thousands of days begun with Him. It has been like a spiritual shower, washing away the dirt of the previous day and starting with a fresh new perspective.

But it wasn't enough. The great peace I got from "loving His law" often got lost in the great pressure of the day's demands. By noon, I was out of touch and, like a gerbil, back on my "wheel."

The next morning my spirit would slow down for another quiet time, then rev up again, leaving that sense of His presence behind. Those blessed interruptions punctuated the stress just enough to give me a taste of peace.

But after my showdown with stress, I knew a taste was not enough. I needed that quiet time calm in the noisy times that filled my day.

I was tired of spiritual binges each morning. As long as I left Him at our morning meeting place, Christ's presence did little to change my responses.

There's a little chorus our children love to sing—one with simple wisdom I was missing:

Love Him in the morning when you see the sun arisin'
Love Him in the evening 'cause He took you through the day
And in the in-between times when you feel the pressure comin'
Remember that He loves you and He promises to stay.*

It was those "in-between times" that were the problem. That early morning closeness had to extend into the heat of the battle.

Protecting the quiet center of time with the Lord was going to require a new discipline of me—*practicing the all-day presence of Christ.*

Five Checkpoints in Our Daily Run

That special sense of going places with Him, doing things with Him, really makes a peaceful difference. I am learning how it can nurture me through phone calls, bill paying, even traffic jams. Frankly, I handle things much better when I am aware Jesus is right there.

He has always wanted it that way. His number-one reason for appointing twelve disciples was not to fill His class or do His work. The Bible says, "He appointed twelve...that they might be *with Him*" (Mark 3:14).

Apparently, it was mission accomplished. When Peter and John were under fire from powerful people three years later, their persecutors saw the difference. "When they saw the courage of Peter and John...they were astonished and they took note that these men had *been with Jesus*" (Acts 4:13).

This with-ness is not a passive state of mystical meditation. It happens on the hoof, all day long. It becomes real as the mind acknowledges that He is indeed "running with us."

These are the five checkpoints for consciously practicing the presence of Christ:

*"All Day Song" by John Fischer, Copyright © 1973 by LEXICON MUSIC, INC. ASCAP All rights reserved. International copyright secured. Used by Special Permission.

- our waking moments
- our running moments
- our surprising moments
- our "nothing" moments
- our fading moments.

Our waking moments set the pace for the day. What fills our minds during those first thirty minutes will play back for many hours to come. While most of us may think we're brain dead in that wake-up fog, there is actually a lot going on up there.

The thoughts may center around the morning news, today's "To Do" list, or the friendly morning disc jockey. It's a mentally lazy time, so sinful and stressful thoughts can slip past sleepy censors.

Christ can be enthroned right in the middle of those waking moments. I try to concentrate my first conscious thoughts in His direction, and I tell Him "good morning!" I review the places I "saw" Him yesterday. If I want music, I listen to songs that will make me think about Him. If I reach for a magazine, I try to reach for one where He is.

Of course, other thoughts creep in, too. But, with a little wakeup concentration, that day's center stage can be captured for Jesus Christ. We can share in King David's energizing morning discovery: "When I awake, I am still with you" (Ps. 139:18).

Most of any day is made up of running moments, both work and play. King Solomon covered our whole agenda when he said, "In *all* your ways *acknowledge* him,/and he will make your paths straight" (Prov. 3:6).

Our first day in geometry taught us that a straight line is the shortest distance between two points. "Straight-line" living will eliminate the twists and turns that inflict stress and get us places faster. This stress-reduction promise calls on us to acknowledge the Lord in every situation.

To acknowledge someone is to notice him, to recognize he's there. Because I'm tired of crooked paths, I have begun to notice Jesus more in the middle of my rat race—between appointments or in the middle of one, as I pick up the phone, in the car, in the grocery line, while emptying the garbage, playing baseball, working late. I'm not pretending He's there. I'm *recognizing* His promised presence.

It is usually impossible for someone to tell I am touching base with my Savior. The rush, the conversation, continues uninterrupted, and I don't drop to my knees in the middle of the office. Acknowledging Him may simply mean a simple "I'm glad You're here, Jesus. Keep me on target." Physically, it sometimes comes out as a deep breath, and I am inhaling more than oxygen.

My wife has taught our three children to acknowledge Christ as they leave for school. In the hustle of lunch money and forgotten homework, her parting words are always, "Have a nice day with Jesus!"

Our family is learning to notice Jesus in the car on our way to church. After the Great Sunday School Race at our house, we need to remember Him on the way. Singing and praying to Him helps us to enter church looking for Him.

It is in life's running moments that we need the perspective of His presence most—and that we tend to forget Him most often. But learning to run with Him changes the way everything and everyone looks. We can relax without ever slowing down.

One of life's adventures is the discovery that God is a God of surprises. Like any good father, He loves to drop "goodies" on His kids unannounced. That's why we look for the Lord in our surprising moments, too.

Unexpected money, an encouraging word, a breakthrough—those are obviously good. No matter who sent the surprise, you can see Jesus looks over the giver's shoulder as the Ultimate Source.

I find it much harder to practice His presence in the less attractive surprises. I may have my day planned down to the minute, then someone needs me and I have to drop everything. I can't waste a minute, yet scores of interruptions chip away at my time. Vacation plans are set, and someone gets sick. I don't like the surprises that change my plans.

But God is in those, too. I have lost count of the times an interruption has turned out to be an inspiration—that my disappointment was His appointment. Some surprises look good today, and some look good after we see the ultimate outcome. But life is newly exhilarating as we look for the God of surprises in the unexpected people and events of each day. They can stress us out, or remind us of Him.

Practicing Christ's presence also involves a kind of time we have all too little of—quiet time. There's nothing like "dead air" to get the staff of a radio station to scramble. That's what they call those embarrassing moments on the air when nothing is happening. The goal of a good radio producer is to see that every minute is filled with effective programming.

It seems as though we hate dead air, too. Most of our life is filled with the clatter of machines and the chatter of people. We don't have the option of quiet when life's necessary noises are broadcasting.

But each of us has some downtime, too—getting ready in the bathroom each morning, waiting for things to happen, traveling. Just like good producers, we fill up most of our dead air with more sound.

If we see our sense of Christ's "with-ness" as a quiet center to guard we will save some of the "nothing moments" for Him.

When my daughter and I get in the car, we reach for different stations, but we both reach instinctively for the radio. My pursuit of peace has taught me to leave the radio off for a change. Those countless hours I spend driving don't all need to be filled, even with Christian radio. Before reaching for the dial, I reestablish contact with my unseen Passenger.

Strangely enough, shower time is becoming worship time. My frayed emotions get a bath, too, when I surround myself with Him. I still devour newspapers and periodicals, but I am learning to carve out a few empty moments by curbing my information appetite a little bit. Sometimes I have to borrow some quiet time from moments always filled before.

So far, I am in little danger of becoming a glassy-eyed mystic, meditating my way through the day. My music, my radio, my reading, my exercising still provide important diversions for me. But I am learning the ministry of guarding a few quiet moments—moments where I simply relax when I think about Him.

If "all's well that ends well," then those last conscious moments of the day are important too. A child's unwinding mind starts to think about monsters in the closet and bugs in the bed. Adults reflect on bigger monsters, like unfinished tasks and unsolved problems.

King David, the proponent of pursuing peace, prescribes a more constructive way to lock up each night. "When you are on your beds, search your hearts and be silent/Offer right sacrifices and trust in the LORD./...I will lie down and *sleep in peace*, for you alone, O LORD, make me dwell in safety" (Ps. 4:4-5, 8).

Occasionally someone will admit sheepishly, "I always fall asleep praying." I can't think of a better way to fall asleep! Now if that's the only time we pray, maybe we should feel sheepish. But if we have been checking in throughout the day, it makes sense to drift off, debriefing the day with Him. David said that slumber send-off would help us to "lie down in peace." There's nothing like a peaceful sleep to set the stage for a peaceful next day!

For three thousand years rabbis have been blessing folks with the benediction God taught Moses. Its familiar, time-tested words go right to the heart of personal peace:

"The LORD bless you and keep you;
The LORD make His face shine upon you
and be gracious to you;
The LORD turn His face toward you
And *give you peace*" (Num. 6:24-26).

It is the Lord's presence—His turning "His face toward you"—that gives peace. In the sea of faces that floods my day, I have too often forgotten to look for the Face that counts most.

But I'm learning. If I really want peace, I cannot afford many days where I run without Christ's with-ness. It begins in that uncompromised cuddle time each morning, time no one else can have. It continues as I acknowledge Him at those five checkpoints—the waking moments, the running moments, the surprising moments, the "nothing" moments, and the fading moments. They provide a real-life plan for practicing the all-day presence of Christ.

A day begun with Him and run with Him provides a powerful shock absorber for the bumpy roads we travel. It is a quiet center that must be carefully guarded on the path to personal peace.

4

Regular Rest and Recovery

New Zealand was as far as I had ever been from home. As much as I was enjoying my teaching assignment there, I was anxious to get home. I had a family to hug and a full catch-up schedule waiting for me.

The day before my scheduled departure, the FAA grounded all DC-10's from flights inside or into the States. They had discovered a dangerous mechanical problem, and every affected aircraft had to be inspected.

Of the three airlines that fly to New Zealand, two use DC-10's. All that was available was one 350-passenger 747 that flew every other night. I was one of 4,000 people stranded a world away from home. My frustration level grew as I reviewed all the commitments I would not be there to keep.

I was graciously offered a furnished house all to myself. I sat alone in a big easy chair the next morning and fumed like an untuned car. Why was I stuck in New Zealand when there was so much to do back home?

Then I remembered something I had frequently told the Lord over the past six months. "Lord, I'm tired and dried up. I really need some rest, some uninterrupted time to be with You. I will slow down if I can just find the time."

The Lord found the time for me, stuck in Auckland, New Zealand! He had grounded me like a human DC-10. It was finally rest time.

I took the hint. I slept long and then spent several uninterrupted hours with my Bible, my pen, and my notebook. God
filled me up with a whole new tankful those two days. I could
tell when I grabbed my legal pad and began to record the
new ideas that were rushing through my mind. For a solid
hour I wrote as fast as I could, filling page after page with
fresh thoughts about every major area of my life. That extended time with the Creator exploded into one of the greatest bursts of creativity I have ever experienced!

The tragedy was that I had waited so long to relax, re-
fresh, and refuel. God had to break the cycle of stress I had
been slaving to serve. He spoke those healing words, "It's
time to rest."

He says that to us often; we just don't listen. We are the
cyclonic creations of a driven society. Our world is a tightly
wound spring that knows no Sabbaths. Our families, our
bodies, our personalities are disintegrating. As people with a
built-in need to rest, we seldom do.

The Missing Drummer

Every August the Pilgrims march at Plymouth again. Actually, over one hundred residents of that historic Massachu-
setts town don Pilgrim clothes and portray those early
settlers.

Our three kids eagerly followed the procession from the
harbor to the church in the center of town. They were most
intrigued by the man who led the march—the Pilgrim drummer. His slow, steady beat set the pace.

"How come they had a drummer?" our youngest asked. I
explained to him how times have changed since 1620. In
those days everyone went to church on Sunday. The drummer's cadence would call the worshipers out of their houses
and into a public procession to church. Anyone who didn't
show broke the law. And the pastor's sermon couldn't possibly be as boring as a day in the stocks.

In fact, a person could be arrested for working on Sunday
as well. The Pilgrims took the idea of a day of rest very seri-

ously. Any violation of this "special day" was prosecuted as "Sabbath breaking."

Yes, times have changed. I have yet to hear a drummer go through our neighborhood on Sunday, calling us to keep the day special. I *have* heard plenty of chain saws and lawn mowers!

For hundreds of years it was rare to find a Sabbath breaker. Today it is rare to find a Sabbath *keeper*. We live in open violation of God's design for a special day each week. We work when we should be worshiping; we run errands when we should be resting.

Our drive has driven out the Sabbath drummer. We are racing to the beat of another drummer, a rhythmic demon whose staccato pace leaves us creatures no time to rest.

A Sabbath day of rest is built into creation. It cannot be cheated against.

"God blessed the seventh day and made it holy, because on it He rested from all the work of creating that He had done" (Gen. 2:3). Created in God's image, we are made to rest after we work. God wrote that right into His laws:

"Six days you shall labor, but on the seventh day you shall rest; even during the plowing season and harvest you must rest" (Exod. 34:21).

God anticipated our saying, "I'll rest after the busy season"..."Even in the plowing time and in harvest you shall rest." He commanded us to protect our time-outs even at the peak of the season!

Regular rest and recovery is not an option in God's plan. There is a price to pay for neglecting it.

The Price of Our Pace

A society without Sabbaths is a culture out of control. The stress damage we see and feel everywhere is the bill come due. Alarms are going off all around us.

Stress used to be just an engineers' word. It described how much weight or pressure a structure could take before it collapsed. Now *people* are collapsing. In a recent cover story on stress (June 6, 1983, p. 48), *Time* magazine traced statistically the toll on our unrested body-buildings.

According to the American Academy of Family Physicians, two-thirds of office visits to family doctors are prompted by stress-related symptoms.

The three best-selling drugs in the country are an ulcer medication (Tagamet), a hypertension drug (Inderal), and a tranquilizer (Valium).

Stress is now known to be a major contributor, either directly or indirectly, to coronary heart disease, cancer, lung ailments, accidental injuries, cirrhosis of the liver, and suicide—six of the leading causes of death in the U.S.

Concludes Dr. Joel Elkes, director of the behavioral medicine program at the University of Louisville: "Our mode of life itself, the way we live, is emerging as today's principal cause of illness."

The Bible describes the body as "a temple of the Holy Spirit" (1 Cor. 6:19). The ancients knew what to do with a temple—treat it special. The way we live is tearing the temple apart.

The emotional toll for our Sabbath breaking is harder to measure, but at least as devastating. Our basic relationships are collapsing in the rubble of child abuse, divorce, and alienation. And suicide grows like an epidemic.

In simple language, we were never meant to live this way. Obviously, something is badly out of balance. Too many bodies, too many lives are being pushed to the breaking point and beyond. The reasons are complex, but they must include our neglect of the Sabbath principle of restorative rest.

In principle, I have long believed these regular time-outs were important. In practice, however, mine have been usually cancelled, postponed, or abbreviated. And even when I stopped, I planned a rest agenda as jampacked as my work agenda.

I don't think I qualify as a workaholic. I enjoy time off too much. But my perception of my responsibilities has made me run right past my rest stops. Somehow I always seem to feel as if I'm behind. I work ninety miles an hour to catch up so I can be with my family. When I'm with my family, I'm going full speed to catch up so I can get my work done. Feeling the deficit in all my responsibilities, I have always been scrambling to pay up.

My Sabbaths became erratic, too far apart to do much good. I saved up for vacation binges, only to find that they could not restore the balance.

I have often told my wife, "I'm tired on a very deep level, honey. It's like there are layers of fatigue, and I never get them all off." That accumulation left me too brittle and buried to handle the stress that goes with my territory.

That fatigue helped me decide "I've had it" with rat-race living. And it helped me start looking for peace.

The pursuit of peace introduced me to another of those five quiet centers. Practicing Christ's presence had given me the first well from which to draw personal peace each day. The Sabbath principle, consistently applied, opened a second reservoir of peace.

Regular rest and recovery provide a stabilizing quiet center. Like every quiet center, it must be protected in the pursuit of peace. If it is not protected, it will be neglected. And stress will keep on winning.

Nibbled Away

Recently a young woman expressed graphically how she felt about her life. "I feel like a cookie," she explained. "So many people have taken bites out of me that there's hardly anything left."

A lot of us know how it feels to be steadily nibbled away. A homemaker fights an unending battle against endless dust, dishes, demands, and dirty clothes. The laundry hamper takes on a life of its own as it reproduces at a rabbit's pace. A student feels every teacher's bite—not to mention Mom, Dad, and up-and-down friends.

The working person feels as if he owes his soul to the company store. The job nibbles away with a list that seems to add a new "undone" for every "done." If the bills are bigger than the paycheck, extra hours or a second job swallow another piece.

And there's a severe leadership shortage in God's work. If you care enough to enlist, you find a deep fulfillment in that first commitment. Since there are so few to help, you get asked again... and again. Eventually there are no nights left without a promise to keep.

We give at the office, at home, at church—finally we give out. Like the cookie lady, there's hardly anything left.

Frankly, tired people are not much fun to be around. Relentless responsibility makes people into robots. They run mechanically, joylessly, from one task to the next, getting it all done but stepping on people as they go. It's not easy to be sensitive when you're all used up.

Unrested people "nuke" their friends and family for insignificant irritations—they have little or no patience. Through tired eyes, small problems look much bigger. Fatigue will bring out a hidden mean streak.

When we don't take time to catch our breath, we just can't carry as much. Our judgment is clouded and we tend to make glandular decisions—the kind we may regret later. Our dark side gains strength and we lose our joy and optimism.

Most damaging of all, we become carriers of stress and guilt and resentment, leaving a trail of tension wherever we go. People who would usually be glad to see us can hardly wait until we're gone.

If there is any rest, it is anything but regular. An occasional vacation or good sleep or day off is just not enough to repair the damage. We take one step forward, and three steps backward. So, as desperately as we need a regular *time-out*, we cry out in frustration, "Where would I *put* it?"

The Myths that Run Us Ragged

Before we can restore a rest-and-responsibility balance, we have to attack some of the myths that keep us running. They cause us to repeatedly say, "I need to stop, but I just can't." And, sure enough, we won't—until God stops us.

1. *The indispensability myth.*

"They just can't get along without me." We become possessed by the belief that it won't get done—or done right—if we don't do it. "Indispensable" people get sick or die every day. Somehow, life continues without them.

Recently some of our friends took a second honeymoon cruise to the Bahamas. Mom found it hard to leave the children—even for such a romantic spot. Could they make it without her? She left meals, emergency phone numbers, and a scrollful of instructions.

She returned a week later to find both children amazingly alive and well. They had not needed to call the emergency numbers; they had not followed all of the instructions; they had not touched half the meals. They *had* left the garbage for the whole week. They may not have taken the high road, but they survived and even thrived while Mom was gone. Mom had a chance to break the chains of the "have-to's" that were strangling the life out of her.

At our house, our Mom is sick with hepatitis right now. Her absence from the center of things has left a big hole. But we're learning new ways to distribute the household load. As much as we love and need her, we are surviving as the song says, "with a little help from our friends."

If what we do at our houses leaves no regular time to regroup, it probably doesn't all need to be done. In fact, some family members might do some important growing if we left some of it for them to do.

If our work has taken control of our life, it may be because we think we are more important than we actually are. The tyranny of the urgent consistently causes late homecomings, takes over "at home" time, and compromises time off.

I hope they can get by without me—they are going to eventually. Something has to give—judgment, attitude, efficiency, health, sanity.

If rest and recovery are ever going to be a quiet center, we first have to step back and see ourselves realistically. It's better for jobs to be undone than for us to be undone. Pursuing peace will mean drawing limits around your life and living within them. Like Kenny Rogers' "Gambler," we must "know when to fold 'em!"

2. *The "you-are-what-you-do" myth*

It begins at a very tender age. Someone asks a little boy, "What do you want to be when you grow up?" We don't look for an answer like, "I want to be sensitive and helpful and friendly." He is supposed to say, "I want to be a doctor...a lawyer...a farmer." We have misled him already. He thinks that what you *do* is who you are.

When those little people grow up, they tend to make their work their highest priority. After all, if I am not my occupation, then who am I?

A workaholic feels he is nobody unless he is working. His work is his worth. So he will drive past all the Sabbath boundaries of life to prove himself. But no effort or achievement will ever be enough. In his wake he will leave people who desperately wanted to be close to him but who could not run fast enough to catch him.

The you-are-what-you-do runner will reach the end of the race alone and unfulfilled. He never had time just to *be*. Without any time for rest and recovery, he has lost large chunks of his humanness.

3. *The dedication myth*

This myth equates nights out with commitment. A committed Christ-follower steps up to service in the Lord's work. He is commended for his fifteen nights in a row at the church and his overloaded schedule. If the spiritual leaders really understood dedication, they would send him right back home a few of those nights.

Someone else could be the chairperson of the Christian education committee, but she is the only Mommy her children have. That man with all those leadership hats is leaving behind a woman he promised to put first always.

People must learn to rest, not just to serve. If they can learn balance, they will be serving for many years. If they don't take regular time-outs, they will play a glorious first quarter, collapse, and hate the game for the rest of their lives. It seems that if the devil can't make us undercommit, he'll make us overcommit.

We are traveling at an unsafe speed today, even without the fuel injected by these no-rest myths. They take away all brakes and leave us with just an accelerator. That's how people crash.

God's own people, the Jews, crashed in ancient time because they refused to rest. The Sabbath principle they ignored covered not only the landowner, but his land as well: "For six years you are to sow your field and harvest the crops, but during the seventh year let the land be unplowed and unused" (Exod. 23:10, 11).

Like many of us, those Old Testament Jews just couldn't slow down. God looked ahead to a time when they would not protect that quiet center of rest and recovery:

Then the land will enjoy its sabbath years all the time that it lies desolate and you are in the country of your enemies; . . . All the time that it lies desolate, the land will have *the rest it did not have* during the sabbath you lived in it (Lev. 26:34-35).

For 490 years, the Jews did not rest the land, for a total of seventy Sabbath years. The Babylonian Empire carried them into captivity and left the land resting for seventy years.

We are built for regular Sabbaths—times of rest and recovery. If we continue to violate our limits, *God will get His Sabbaths*, whether that rest comes through an accident, an injury, an illness, or a closed door. He would much rather we choose to rest. And it is a deliberate choice.

Slowing Down

We have to plan to rest, or we won't rest. Those plans protect this revitalizing quiet center.

We need to plan daily rest. A short night's sleep can be balanced with a full one the next night. Sleep is the balance wheel of our health and personality. Recent studies show that the hours before midnight are the best sleep. Protecting our daily rest might mean sacrificing late-night TV or reading. The discipline that turns out that light pays off in clear thinking and pleasant disposition that next day. I am beginning to learn that adequate sleep might leave me fewer work hours, but they will be much better hours!

Second, we need to plan for *weekly* rest. That means marking a day off in the same dark ink used for appointments and meetings. If someone asks for that time, you learn to say, "I'm sorry, I already have a commitment." That commitment is to rebuild self and family.

Third, we need to plan *extended* rest—weekends and vacations. Location is not the most important factor. It's *change*! Our early vacations as a family ran us from one tourist spot to another each day. Afterward, we needed a break to recover from our vacation. Running is what our lives are like all year. Now we have learned to settle into one quiet place and just become a part of that little corner of the world. We explore, buy the local newspaper, get lost on back roads. Our rest times are as unplanned as the rest of our life is planned. The change refreshes and restores.

Some people save up all their Sabbathing for one or two grand and glorious vacations each year. By the time their bodies and family members wind down enough to rest, it's time to come home. Rest and recovery binges don't work! Daily and weekly time-outs missed can't be replaced with a make-up super-Sabbath every few months.

When I finally began to get serious about the connection between peace and rest, I had to buy a new datebook. The old one showed me one day at a time; I couldn't see what I was doing to myself and my family over a thirty-day period. Now I look at a full month before I make any new commitment. It helps me balance a stretch of time-in with a compensating time-out.

A Day to Keep Special

The golden moment of the motion picture industry in recent years was a movie called "Chariots of Fire." On the surface, it was the story of the 1924 Paris Olympics. In reality, it was a tribute to a man with unshakable convictions. His name was Eric Liddell.

Liddell was Great Britain's best in the hundred-meter event, but one day he refused to run. His Christian convictions had led him to keep Sunday special. Much to his dismay, he learned en route to Paris that he would have to run his event on Sunday. His decision to "keep the Sabbath holy" rocked the Olympics.

In a last-minute shift, Eric Liddell competed two days later in the four-hundred-meter event—one he had not prepared for. In an unforgettable scene from "Chariots of Fire," an American Olympian slips a handwritten note to Liddell. Having watched with respect this display of conviction, the American quotes the Bible: "Those who honor Me I will honor" (1 Sam. 2:30).

Eric Liddell went home from Paris with the Olympic gold, and the reward of God. He dared to keep the Lord's Day special. Sixty years later another generation honored Eric Liddell's story with gold, the Academy Award for "Best Movie." Although Eric Liddell had been dead for forty years, his life was still speaking.

In a sense, Eric Liddell helped me write this book. Writing time has been hard to come by in my overstuffed life. Several blocked-out weekends were the key to its completion. On the first weekend, I faced a frustrating conflict. I really needed Sunday for writing. The days were running out like sand out of an hourglass.

But we have been trying to keep Sunday special around

our house, especially since we started pursuing peace. If I
did not work on Sunday, however, I was sure I was pursuing
stress. How would I ever finish without using those precious
Sundays (after church, of course)?

With my children watching my values on the line, I put
away my typewriter for Sunday. We went to church, enjoyed
a relaxing family dialogue over dinner, romped on the local
playground, went for a ride, and had some quality family devotions.

That "those who honor Me" note was right on target. I
went back to the typewriter the next day, and I wrote more in
one day than I had ever been able to do in *two*! It was as if
God were pouring the thoughts right through my brain and
into my fingers.

I don't suppose we will ever become legalistic about Sunday. I don't plan to hire a drummer for church time. But
when you start to keep the Lord's Day special, you begin to
feel this was meant to be what's normal. The turbulent body
and spirit start to stabilize. So we try to avoid buying on
Sunday, if at all possible, as well as refraining from doing
homework and chores. Jesus said it was okay to get an ox out
of a ditch on the Sabbath and we do occasionally have to rescue oxen. But that is the exception. The rule is that Sunday
is special.

Above all else, it is a day to stop for concentrated time to
admire God. Going to church can be, in itself, just another
obligation or activity. But if approached with an appetite for
worshiping the Lord, church is the right place to be.

The Scriptures consistently attach special value to God's
people getting together. Nothing should be allowed to erode
a family's consistent involvement in a corporate celebration
of God. Even if most other folks don't seem to be there to
worship, we can if we go looking for the Lord.

Something about remembering God's majesty corrects
what a week's pressure has distorted. David exulted:

In His temple all cry, "Glory!"
The LORD sits enthroned over the flood;
The LORD is enthroned as King forever.
The LORD gives strength to His people;
The LORD blesses His people with peace (Ps. 29:9-11).

When we get excited about the Kingship of Christ, we start to relax our souls. Out of worship comes peace.

The Lord gave us a day to give back to Him. When we do, our tightly wound lives get a chance to rest.

The oak tree by the rampaging river doesn't have a chance without its unshakable root system.

Peace—the deep down calm we cry for—doesn't stand a chance without nonnegotiable quiet centers. They begin with that uncompromised time with the Lord each day; they are restored through regular rest and recovery. These quiet centers network with three others we are about to explore. Together they send roots deep enough to anchor anyone, anywhere.

5

Guarding Your Huddle Time

Sitting on the picturesque porch of a lakefront cottage, peace comes easily. There I was, enjoying the stress-free Adirondack air with my Bible open on my lap. Day after day, I had been pursuing peace through God's Word. The more I read, the more dissatisfied I became with the life-twisting merry-go-round I had come to accept as normal.

But my magic kingdom days of vacation were running out. I wondered if I could really make peace a lifestyle. I was so tired of preaching peace but practicing pressure. In my urgent search for inner calm, God has shown me another way to live.

The porch is gone, but the peace has remained. My schedule has not slowed down, but my spirit has. No sooner had I made a commitment to insist on peace than stress brought out the heavy artillery.

• My wife has had three dangerous illnesses in the last nine months.

• The staff for whom I am responsible went through a major upheaval.

• Our daughter started high school.

• Our son started junior high school with a badly broken arm.

• We faced a decisive deadline in the legal tangle resulting from a serious accident.

- Paychecks for our staff were delayed.
- The kitchen floor and the back stairs fell apart.

All these surprises came in right on top of my already relentless schedule full of speaking, counseling, managing, radio, nonstop meetings, and daddying. The peace has stood the test. To be sure, my old high-pressure, high-pitched responses still surface, but I retreat quickly to the new peace I have chased and found. This tranquillity is anything but theoretical or passive. It is the product of a daily insistence that we choose the peace alternative.

The secret is in my quiet centers, right from the pages of the Bible. The peace promises are attached to them. If those centers were the result of some deep breathing exercises and mystical meditation, they would never turn the tide in my pragmatic daily whirlwind.

Quiet centers are concrete commitments to concrete action. To seek peace is to insist on these five personal priorities—and to protect them from the encroachments of busyness.

The pressure doesn't feel nearly as great as it used to. I have tasted the eye of the hurricane. I do not want to go back to being a part of the storm. That determination makes the quiet centers worth fighting for. Uncompromised time with the Lord and regular rest and recovery provide the perspective that produces personal peace. But *inter*personal peace is drawn from other wells.

Time for Each Other

I went after many goals in college: good grades, leadership positions, ministry opportunities. But I went after nothing quite so energetically as a girl named Karen. I had to run hard—there were a lot of other guys in the race! The good news is that she was in my arms at the finish line, and she has been there ever since.

We spent a lot of time together when this "froggy went a courtin'." The magnets inside us would not allow us to be apart long. We talked about all the unfolding feelings and events of our lives. When I made my vows to her on our wedding day, I was sure those "together times" would be more and better than ever.

Then high tide hit our lives, and it has never receded. We both worked and our home became a "Grand Central Station" for teen-agers. Three children needed lots of time. The phone stayed so busy we almost lost it in a meltdown. The pushes and pulls have taken their toll on "together time."

As I look back over our first twenty years, I see how many days slipped through our hands without our touching each other's hearts. When we have our time, we both can handle the day's pressures with calm and confidence. In fact, we can even head off a few of them! When that time keeps getting crowded out, a vital quiet center has been violated. Quality communion with your closest friend is part of the way you're created!

It began with Adam (just about everything did!). You would think his "good life" could not have gotten "gooder." His address was Paradise, his job was to be in charge of the entire operation, he was friends with God. Yet, in spite of all this, God said Adam was "alone" (Gen. 2:18). He was missing the companionship, the partnership of a peer. "The LORD God said, 'It is not good for the man to be alone. I will make a helper suitable for him' " (Gen. 2:18).

That need was met by one of God's most dramatic creative acts:

"Then the LORD God made a woman from the rib He had taken out of the man, and He brought her to the man...

"For this reason a man will leave his father and mother and be united to his wife, and they will become one flesh" (Gen. 2:22, 24).

We are designed to *live in active partnership with someone we love.* Life lived alone is too big to handle. A child's peace depends on his closeness to his parents; a single adult's peace requires a "soul mate" friend; a husband or wife's peace is proportionate to the depth of their friendship.

While marriage is not the only form of life partnership, for most people it is the *highest* form. For many couples, however, their friendship has turned to frustration. The promise of intimacy and communication is buried under the pressures and demands that have smothered it.

Some marriages end with the "bang" of a divorce; more end with the "whimper" of slow drift and growing silence. God's gift to enhance peace becomes—through the sin of neglect—an almost unbearable disappointment.

The pathway to personal peace includes a new commitment to living in partnership. A football team who seldom huddled wouldn't make it to the Dust Bowl, let alone the Super Bowl. In the same way, a husband and wife must protect their regular huddle—no matter how busy they are playing the game.

Uncompromised time with a life partner is a quiet center too precious to neglect. That time is, in terms of the ravages of stress, both an ounce of prevention and a pound of cure.

Hers

Cuddle time with the Lord is the time to listen to the most important voice in Heaven; huddle time with a life partner is a time to listen to the most important voice on earth. The marriage commitment implies putting the partner first. That's almost impossible to do if he or she cannot get on your agenda regularly.

A woman without that husband "huddle time" unconsciously starts a buildup that will one day blow like a volcano. If she consistently feels unheard, she will eventually feel unloved. And that is a dangerous state. The Bible warns "Under three things the earth trembles, under four it cannot bear up:/...*an unloved woman* who is married" (Prov. 30:21, 23).

A wife may be loved by her husband, but she may not feel loved. She craves a oneness that can only be built through daily debriefings.

When a man wonders how he ended up married to a nag, the mirror might be the first place to look for an answer. A woman who feels unheard will talk louder, longer, and more often. She is beating on the door to her husband's heart. He didn't answer when she knocked gently.

When a woman wonders how she ended up married to a silent partner, she might try the mirror, too. Men sometimes withdraw from communicating when they consistently get frustrating results. He talks. She interrupts, criticizes, acts bored, uses what he says as ammunition later, and violates his confidences. He stops talking.

His

A man without that "huddle time" unravels as surely as his wife does. He just fills up his life with other things. Thus, it takes him longer to notice what they both have lost.

Home is the place where he was meant to unload burdens and load up on encouragement. A man has a need for closeness that only his Eve can satisfy. If he keeps missing the huddle, he will get "life partner" close to the boys, the blonde, the bartender, or the business. In so doing, he will sow the seeds of his own destruction. It is a wise man who protects time to share with his wife. She can see things he may never see.

One intriguing trait of the male species is that he never admits he is lost. The one-hour trip has already taken three hours, but Dad insists he knows exactly where he is going. Mom suggests that he stop and ask for directions at a gas station; Dad suggests that Mom keep knitting.

Karen and I have developed a fuel-saving alternative. I am the pilot, she is the navigator. I have the wheel, Karen has the map. We are both very good at what we do. We get places so much faster when we fly together like that.

Families live more peacefully when a husband realizes that God gave him a wife to be his navigator. In their goal-oriented drive for conquest, men can get lost. Women are often the value clarifiers of the home. They remind men that

people are more important than things, that the children
need more love or more control, that the family is drifting
spiritually.

The Bible describes the woman whose "husband has full
confidence in her/and lacks nothing of value" (Prov. 31:11).
This emotionally rich man has a wife who "watches over the
affairs of her household/...who fears the LORD" (Prov.
31:27, 30).

A man is *made* to need his partner. It is no wonder he gets
lost when she gets crowded out of his life.

Avoiding Avalanches!

Wedding-day intentions are noble. The couple expects to
talk regularly, to keep up on each other's lives. Years later
they realize how many days they have been *around* each
other, but not *with* each other.

There is a facet of female chemistry that causes her to let
time together slide. She protects what she loves. When a
woman sees her husband is under a lot of pressure, she
doesn't want to add to it. She says, "The poor guy is busy
right now. He doesn't need my problems, too. It can wait."
At times, it is a loving response to wait until his load is
lighter. But as days become weeks, the postponed agendas
pile up and the volcano starts to rumble.

Karen and I have had some good laughs over the occasional avalanches at our house. You might suspect they come
from our children's closets; actually they come from too
many postponed huddles. Either I have been "too busy"
every time Karen has asked for time or she has been too kind
to push her high-flying husband.

Finally, I respond to her "Can I talk to you about something, honey?" approach. Like a loose thread on a sweater, it
starts slowly and then really starts to unravel. Every item she
shares with me reminds her of another. Before long, I'm buried in an avalanche! My anguished cry for help asks, "Why
did you wait so long to tell me all this? I can't handle so

much at once. Why didn't you tell me about these things as they came up?"

She doesn't need to answer. I already know. She tried, but I was travelling too fast to hear, or I did not leave any time where she could even try.

When a woman consistently decides not to "bother" her husband, she is doing him no favor. Either her concerns will bother him when they are small enough to handle or big enough to bury him.

That is why the Bible so wisely counsels us, "Do not let the sun go down while you are still angry, and do not give the devil a foothold" (Eph. 4:26-27).

We are meant to debrief daily. If we are "unavailable for comment" too many days, we give the enemy a destructive edge.

The make-up of the male features a trait that keeps him out of the huddle. He avoids situations where he does not feel competent. A man is sure of himself in his work; he is usually unsure of his skills in deeply personal relationships.

Men tend to base their relationships on activities—sports, job, politics. Women tend to base their relationships on personal feelings, an area most men are uncomfortable discussing.

So men keep running when there is serious talking to do. Once again, it all started with Adam. When God came to talk after that first sin, Adam grabbed Eve's hand and ran. Adam is still running from substantial conversation, even with Eve. He thinks he can do without it. He's wrong.

The "huddle time" as a quiet center will remain safe only through the initiating leadership of the man and the gentle persistence of the woman. To pursue time together is to pursue personal peace.

It's easy to tell what's really important in my life—just look at my datebook. It is packed with time I have blocked out for appointments, speaking engagements, and meetings. If my wife is really important to me, she will make it into the book. Her "importants" are on a calendar; I should have some slots there. Once a week seems to be the minimum for a solid, extended sit-down. Our commitment to huddle time is just words without a scheduled spot for it.

Some of those times need to be good, old-fashioned dates. We would rather go out to dinner than to a concert or a show. We need to talk, not always watch someone else talk. And our year needs to include at least a couple of occasions when we "run away from home" together. A weekend without the children rekindles romance and allows time enough to talk about the future, not just the present.

But dates and weekends are no substitute for the foundation of marital communication—staying in touch daily. That time together does not have to be long, but it must be consistent. At our home we call it avalanche prevention.

Building the Ultimate Friendship

A marriage partner can be a best friend through the huddle. It is much more than just a problem-solving session. Bonds are built as together time is used for three essential priorities.

1. The ultimate priority is praying with each other. The depth of prayer is more important than the length. This is not primarily "bless the missionaries" or "help the building fund," you kneel together to turn over deep fears and frustrations and feelings; to articulate dreams; to wage war for a struggling or wandering child; to get His perspective on the down-home material needs of your family; to confess the sinful attitude or action you struggle with.

The leadership of the Spirit in prayer often causes us to stumble on a liberating insight or a creative solution. Expressing something to God may be easier than expressing it directly to a partner. But preaching when praying—"Lord, open George's eyes to how stubborn he's been"—won't help communication.

2. The second priority needs to be *planning with each other*—getting out that datebook or calendar and reviewing each

other's commitments. A lot of stressful surprises can be headed off that way: "You're going *where* next Tuesday night?" With schedules in hand, set the next few times together. Make a list of items that need mutual attention.

Planning goes far beyond schedules, of course. There are decisions to be researched, evaluated, and settled...how to handle Jimmy's "bad influence" friends; spending priorities to get out of debt; a step-by-step plan for house repairs; a way to control the phone or the TV; how to allocate giving to God's work.

Decisions have a way of making themselves. The longer the "leadership team" waits to handle it, the shorter the list of options. Regular talk time reduces the stressful results of decisions made too late—or never.

3. When it's huddle time, the third priority is *providing a harbor for each other*. All day long we mask deep feelings from the children, people at work, friends. Time spent together consistently helps develop trust.

The person who sees you physically unclothed should be able to see you emotionally naked, too. Huddle time with the life partner is a place to unload, to unmask, to laugh, to cry, to brag a little, to work out grudges, to be at the end of your rope. While you should not *take* out pain on your partner, you should *let* it out there. The soul-mate needs to feel that harboring safety of love—no rejection, no matter what.

Together time with your life partner is an investment. The dividends are generous.

Close parents have confident kids. They are marching to one drumbeat because the drummers have practiced together. A child becomes a rebel when he is confused by marching to the beat of two different drums. He glows and grows in a predictable, stable climate—the kind that comes from Mom's and Dad's knowing each other intimately.

Huddling parents are also cuddling parents. The trust and tenderness that comes through communication opens up a whole new sexual adventure for a married couple. The Bible uses the word *know* to describe sexual love. The more you know each other in every area of life, the more exciting it is to say "I *know* you" in each other's arms.

And the greatest dividend of all is that infinite friendship—that very deep sense of lovedness. In the security of that relationship, you can handle high tides. Joys are doubled; burdens are halved.

Single—But Not Alone

The apostle Paul was not married; neither was he alone. His letters are filled with references to his life-partner network.

He told us about the mother of Rufus, "who has been a mother to me, too" (Rom. 16:13). Timothy "as a son with his father he has served with me in the work of the gospel" (Phil. 2:22). After a period of separation from his "son," Paul said: "Recalling your tears, I long to see you, so that I may be filled with joy" (2 Tim. 1:4).

In Paul's darkest moments, Onesiphorus "refreshed" him (2 Tim. 1:16). To the believers in Rome he wrote: "By God's will I may come to you with joy and together with you be refreshed" (Rom. 15:32).

Paul was a tower of spiritual and emotional strength. If any Christian could have "gone it alone," surely he was the man. Yet he nurtured and needed that peer partnership.

To be single is not to be limited to some second-class love experience. The principles that govern a married quiet center will build an unmarried one, too. Parents (both biological and honorary), brother or sister, soul-deep friends—these are the life partnerships single persons protect. That time, that closeness is to be guarded as a nonnegotiable in the pursuit of peace. The God who made us to need people will give us the people we need.

Years ago I was captivated with a movie title, "The Heart Is a Lonely Hunter." It was never meant to be that way. God built us to buddy up. The more we dance to the driving beat of stress, the more we dance alone. No one can run fast enough to get close to us. The pressure squeezes the people who love us most right out of our lives.

But a line can be drawn. A "peace hunter" doesn't have to be lonely. That's why Paul told Timothy to pursue peace "along with those who call on the Lord out of a pure heart" (2 Tim. 2:22). The line we draw refuses any deadline, any position, any have-to that will cost "with" time.

Like Adam and Eve, it is not good for us to be alone.

6

Consistent Family Faith Times

When a young married couple impulsively says, "Let's *go* somewhere," they only have to think about it once. When they have a baby to take along, they have to think at least twice.

Lisa was our first baby, and the poor little girl was practically mummified every time we took her out on a cold day. By the time we wrapped her up in sweaters, pants, booties, and blankets, we had no time left to go anywhere! Of course, as every parent knows, blanketed babies are only the beginning.

As the kids grow, so does the pile of coats, scarves, gloves, boots, and foul-weather gear. The more stormy the weather, the more carefully we insure their being properly dressed for it.

Every morning we send our children out the door into stormy weather—into a morally and emotionally turbulent world. I watch them go, knowing they may face a confusing shower of put-downs, pressures, temptations, profanity, attractive lies, and personality pollution. Stress comes dressed in jeans and sneakers, not just in aprons and three-piece suits. Our children feel the wear and tear against peaceful living, too.

In Sunday school we used to sing, "Be careful, little eyes, what you see; be careful, little ears, what you hear." That's good counsel. But no matter how careful our children are, their eyes and ears are still bombarded with toxic moral waste and relentless pressure to perform.

We cannot go with them to hold the umbrella. We can be sure they are dressed for the weather.

It isn't enough, you see, that *I* am protected with stabilizing inner peace. I want it for my children, too. After all, they have been marked by their father's stress. Shouldn't they be marked now by the peace alternative?

The verse over the kitchen sink told me how to include my family in the pursuit of peace. My wife put it there a long time ago, and it finally registered. God's reassuring promise is:

All your sons will be taught by the LORD, and *great will be your children's peace* (Isa. 54:13).

Relief and responsibility: those two feelings sweep over me as that promise penetrates my heart. I experience the relief of knowing God's hand is busy in the kids' lives. I find myself returning to this confidence often as I watch them sleep or watch them leave.

But there is responsibility here, too. Peace must be *pursued* for our children as well as for us adults. As Mom and Dad, we create the climate, the structure in which the Lord's lessons can be taught.

Another quiet center needed to be built and protected—*consistent family faith times*.

Watching the Same Channel

Twelve-year-old boys have a way of getting to the point. At least, our twelve-year-old boy does. Karen had recently celebrated her milestone fortieth birthday. She actually had forgotten it, but Doug had not. One day he stopped her with, "Hey, Mom," and then observed with widening eyes, "do you realize that you have been alive *14,662 days*!"

Being forty is one thing...but living 14,662 days?

We have had approximately 4,380 days to train up Doug

"in the way he should go"—more days with his sister, fewer with his brother. How many of those days have included substantial teaching about the Lord? Not enough.

In reordering my life around peace, I knew to pursue it effectively as a family we had to do better with the days we had left. I also knew that a daily time of formal family devotions probably would not work in our dizzy lives. Our five lives can be like bumper cars at the carnival—we step on the gas each morning, go full speed ahead in five different directions, and then occasionally run into each other. I was prepared to make a commitment to family faith time, but I wanted one that could be consistent and meaningful.

Our kids have learned well their lessons in being busy and involved, and I'm afraid it was caught, not taught. It's almost as if we had five different TV sets in our lives, one for each member of the family. We each watch a different channel. I'm tuned to the news; Mom is watching something educational; the children are watching a love story, a ballgame, and cartoons, respectively.

Family faith time means that I make sure that we are all together once a day, tuned to the same spiritual channel. Our family quiet center is some time each day when we all focus on the Lord Jesus together.

The Buck Stops Here

The weather had changed for the Jewish people, and Moses had to be sure his "kids" were dressed for it. For forty years, they had lived on little in the wilderness, basically insulated from anti-God ideas by their separation from the world around them. Now they were about to move on into their Promised Land. They would have to live for the Lord among the plush affluence and the pagan influence of Canaan—much like our children do today. Moses put the responsibility for spiritual health right where it belonged:

"Remember today that your children were not the ones who saw and experienced the discipline of the LORD your God: His majesty, His mighty hand, His outstretched arm;...It was not your children who

saw what He did for you in the desert until you arrived at this place,
...but it was your own eyes that saw all these great things the LORD has
done.... *Teach them to your children*, talking about them when you sit at
home and when you walk along the road, when you lie down and when
you get up" (Deut. 11:2, 5, 7, 19).

The Bible charges parents directly to give their children the
God they know!

"Teach" is the assignment, and everyday life is the setting. This is natural, spontaneous faith to be sure, but sys-
tematically communicated.

The responsibility for family faith belonged first to Adam.
Nowhere did God explain to Eve about the forbidden fruit,
yet she knew the word of God when the serpent came. God
told Adam, and He expected Adam to tell Eve. When the
Lord visited them after their disobedience, "The LORD God
called to the *man*, 'Where are you?' " (Gen. 3:9).

Although Eve had committed the first sin, God held
Adam responsible. Nothing has changed. In God's eyes, the
spiritual buck still stops with the man of the house. Paul
said: "Fathers, do not exasperate your children; instead,
bring them up in the training and instruction of the Lord"
(Eph. 6:4).

My son Doug and I were reminiscing the other day about
his first lessons in playing baseball. He is so skillful today
that it's hard for me to remember back to that little four-
year-old guy with the plastic ball and bat. I stood five feet
from him then, and he chopped awkwardly at the ball. Gently, by word and demonstration, I showed him how to stand,
how to swing evenly, how to follow through. He responded
well to that training. Today I pitch as fast as I can and he hits
those balls accurately—and very hard.

Dads make good coaches, and it's no secret. Bringing up
your children "in the training and admonition of the Lord"
is basically coaching on a spiritual level. Dad does not have
to be a world-class theologican or scholar. God gives the
coach's cap to Dad, and he simply passes on the faith.

If Dad is not on God's team yet, Mom can still establish

family faith time. We know that because Paul's most trusted associate, Timothy, was raised in a spiritually divided home. Only his mother knew Christ. And Paul believed she did an admirable job of coaching: "I have been reminded of your (Timothy's) sincere faith, which first lived in your grandmother Lois and in your mother Eunice and, I am persuaded, now lives in you also" (2 Tim. 1:5).

And mother Eunice apparently did not waste many days of her son's life: "From *infancy* you have known the holy Scriptures" (2 Tim. 3:15).

If our children are ever going to enjoy what the Bible calls great peace, they must be taught by the Lord. If they are ever going to be taught by the Lord, it must come through Mom and Dad. Anything the church, the youth leader, or the Christian school can do for our children is usually supplemental. Family faith time is clearly nonnegotiable. But it will never happen until Dad (or Mom, if he is not a Christian) decides it must happen.

The Coach Convenes the Team

Because we men like to stick to areas we're good in, we are sometimes slow to step up to the position of spiritual headcoach. If we wait until we are sure of ourselves as a family spiritual leader, our family will never be properly nurtured.

At our house, our three children have enough musical instruments on hand for the Hutchcraft Philharmonic—piano, organ, trumpet, flute, piccolo, saxophone, clarinet, and guitar. In every case, their first month on a new instrument has driven us right up the wall. The moans and slurs, squeaks and scratches in the house motivate me to get a lot more yard work done. But for all the bad notes, we're sure glad they have kept playing. They had to start playing like beginners, or they never would have started at all!

A father does not have to be perfect to start convening his family for faith times. He is a failure in God's eyes only if he doesn't try!

As I began to realize that this quiet center needed to be

shaped up in our house, I struggled with how. With five busy lives, it was easy to think of reasons it couldn't be done. But it was not negotiable. So I looked for a commitment that would come down somewhere between the ideal of everyday organized daily devotions and the reality of our bumper-car lives.

Since our lives are really days, I determined we should not waste another day. Not another twenty-four-hour period would slide by without our focusing on the Lord together. That could happen for us if I made two commitments: a *formal family faith time* at least twice a week, and an *informal family faith time* at least *once a day*.

The formal team meetings must, of course, be scheduled in advance by every team member. One may be on the weekend, taking advantage of a less demanding pace. Workday/ schoolday times may best revolve around a relaxed dinner hour that everyone is committed to reserving. Perhaps it should come later in the evening at a prearranged hour when everyone plans a time-out in his activities. Phone calls will be returned in a few minutes; drop-in visitors will be included in your get-together. The scheduling of these two time-outs can be flexible each week; the frequency is not.

A Changing Menu

Our boys love the pizza at a certain restaurant at the Jersey Shore. Recently, they spent a week at the shore, which gave them an unexcelled gourmet opportunity. Since I left my "Basic Four Food Groups" chart at home, I let them eat their dream pizza too many times. As much as they love that stuff, they were dog-tired of it by the end of the week. Even our favorite food can get tiresome if we have it all the time!

That is why we need to vary the menu when we feed our family spiritually. Since the big meals are twice weekly, a little creativity can be put into the fare. Tell a Bible story, dramatize a parable... illustrate a practical principle from an incident one of you have experienced...share the reading of a Christian biography. Have each person share an insight from his "cuddle time" with the Lord (that's where spiritual diaries help!). Follow a thought through the Bible (how about peace?). Brainstorm a practical application each one can try, based on verses studied.

Our kids seem to remember the object lessons best. One day I brought a red rubber ball to our family faith time. We tossed it around for a while. Then I said, "Let's imagine that this ball is an insult or a put-down. Now throw it at me." I caught it. But I did not return it. "I feel like throwing this back," I confessed. "I've been taught to return what people throw to me, but I won't." The focus of our Bible study turned out to be: "Do not repay anyone evil for evil....Do not be overcome by evil, but overcome evil with good" (Rom. 12:17, 21).

We learned together that day about the throw you *don't return*—the hurt someone has hurled your way. The idea came as I simply asked myself, "What physical object could I use to show this somewhat abstract principle?"

Family faith time is more than Bible study. It's also prayer for real, personal things; a review of how well we have lived, what we have learned since last time, the raising and answering of spiritual questions, the singing of a favorite song.

To protect the quiet center of two family faith times each week is to sow great peace in your children—and in yourself.

The Classroom of Everyday Life

A formal family faith time may not be possible every day, but you can stop to notice Jesus. In a sense, a day when we have not touched Christ together is a day wasted.

Moses told the Israelite parents to talk about the Lord "when you sit at home and when you walk along the road, when you lie down and when you get up" (Deut. 11:19). The First Church of Your House is the perfect place to teach in the classroom of everyday life.

The Master's moments are all throughout a family's living together. A parent need only train his eye to recognize them. Informal family faith times come naturally out of:

1. *The needy moment*

Money is tight—We share a verse or Bible story about God's supply and turn the need over to the Heavenly Father.

A decision is confusing—We review God's leadership in past choices, read a passage about His guidance, and join hands to get a shared sense of leading.

School starts tomorrow—Gather around the nervous young scholar, put your hands on him, and pray around the circle.

A family member is sick—We can share from the Bible one special thing God does for people when they are down. Then we pray around the sick person, recognizing the Lord's personal presence in that room.

2. *Teachable moments*

One family member's experience today becomes the lens through which we all can look at a biblical principle. A son's frustration over playground injustice became our setting to learn about not letting the sun go down on anger. A camping trip underscored God's majesty when we read that: "He stretches out the heavens like a canopy,/and spreads them out *like a tent* to live in" (Isa. 40:22).

A question about nuclear war, spawned by watching the evening news, is answered with an impromptu discussion of the return of Christ. If we *look* for teachable moments, we find them!

3. *Dinner moments*

Family dinner should be the sacrament of Christian family life. That takes a lot of cooperation between the cook and the commuter, but it's worth it. A relaxed review of the "goods" and "bads" of each person's day provides the grist for acknowledging Christ's presence and applying His principles.

4. *Broken moments*

There is a wall between two family members. An apology, a confession, a need to forgive or be forgiven, an appeal for help to change are deeply spiritual moments. The family can touch the Lord in a special way if together they make a wall into a bridge.

The classroom of everyday life is the most powerful learning climate on earth. No one else could possibly serve as the faculty other than Dad and Mom. They are the only ones close enough to do it.

Families who find the Lord together daily can find each other, too. Without this Super-Glue the natural tendency of accelerating personal lives will be to fly apart. Like centrifugal force, stress spins each of us to a lonely place at the outside of the circle.

Because our lives are so full, we can't seem to fit in consistent family faith times. Because our lives are so full, we must!

The storm outside your house will intensify, not subside. But you can build your own little island of sanity inside your house if each day you will *focus on the Lord together.*

Every peace-pursuing family needs a Nehemiah. He led an extended "family" of Jewish refugees through a high-pressure season of life. They had massive responsibilities— the rebuilding of the wall of Jerusalem; a tight deadline; and pagan enemies all around them. It was difficult to keep the family close when their daily assignments took them a hundred different directions. Sounds like a family I know very well.

But Nehemiah announced his "stay together" plan:

"The work is extensive and spread out, and we are widely separated....Wherever you hear the sound of the trumpet, join us there" (Neh. 4:19-20).

If we feel our families getting "spread out and widely separated," we must rise to the Nehemiah Challenge. At different times, in different places, the trumpet of peace can bring the family together around Christ. Peace comes to live in a family whose ear is always tuned to the sound of that "come-together" trumpet!

7

Reprogramming Your Personality

For centuries men had looked at the moon, crooned about the moon, and dreamed about the moon. The Apollo astronauts walked on the moon. We who were eyewitnesses to history will never forget the thrill of Neil Armstrong's "one small step for man," and the other steps that followed.

Of course, Neil Armstrong didn't really look like himself. He was totally wrapped in that modern-day armor called a space suit. The moon is an environment hostile to humans. Unequipped astronauts would have died in an instant of lunar exposure. Why? No oxygen! That big pack on their backs was the margin of survival.

If the Apollo explorers had depended on their surroundings for their lives, they would have died on the moon. Instead, they depended on the *life-support system they carried with them!*

While pursuing peace, I was brought back to an often neglected life-support system. Breathing the thin, polluted air of my surroundings was leaving me gasping. I was drawing a new balance from quiet centers like cuddle time with the Lord, huddle time with my wife, family faith times, and Sabbath rests. But I needed a support system that I could carry with me through the wear and tear of the day—something highly mobile, highly dependable.

It was in Jesus' greatest peace promise that I rediscovered it again:

"Peace I leave with you; my peace I give you. I do not give to you as the world gives. Do not let your hearts be troubled and do not be afraid" (John 14:27).

I had known that passage for years, but I had not protected the wells in which He puts His peace. One of those wells is described in the sentence that immediately precedes this promise. Locked up in the context is that final quiet center I needed, the One I could carry with me. Jesus said:

"The Holy Spirit...will teach you all things and will *remind you of everything I have said to you*. Peace I leave with you" (John 14:26-27).

The peace promise came at a moment when the disciples' lives were falling apart. Jesus had just announced He was leaving; the soldiers were on their way to arrest Jesus; the Cross was hours away; they had just been warned to expect rejection and persecution. Yet the Lord was guaranteeing peace.

Obviously, Jesus' peace has nothing to do with how things are going—things were utterly out of hand when He promised it. The Christian who says he is all right "under the circumstances" has no business under them! We can clear the clutter of troubles for our hearts, no matter how much change, rejection, or confusion there is!

The key is in that reminding work of the Holy Spirit. At the very moment of trouble, He will bring to center stage the words of Jesus, but He cannot remind us of what we *never knew*! Remembering His words brings poise under pressure.

The quiet center we carry with us is the Scripture we have, planted in our personality.

Better Air

My son and I had both had one of those "bad days." My tension from work and his tension from school collided in hard words about chores that needed to be done. In my busy moments I had learned ways to shorten arguments—and win them. It required only a cutting remark that produced guilt and surrender. Stressed-out parents can crush a fragile spirit.

I was just about to win with my ugly weapon. Then the computer brought up something from my memory banks. On the screen flashed a reminder from the Holy Spirit— "Do not let any unwholesome talk come out of your mouths, but *only what is helpful for building others up* according to their needs..." (Eph. 4:29).

What I was about to say would not have been helpful for building up my son. It would tear him down. The air around me was poisoned with tension, I chose not to breathe it. I breathed instead the inner oxygen supplied by the Holy Spirit from a verse our family had just memorized. I hugged my son instead of hurting him with my words. Peace had won. The quiet center was working! The words of Jesus had given me *restraint*.

On another overheated day last fall, I was experiencing the truth of "when it rains, it pours." Our corporate income, for which I am ultimately responsible, had slowed drastically enough to cause delays in our payroll. Our son was at home, depressed over the pain of a broken arm and the next six sportsless months. In addition, I had just returned home from an overseas trip to a pile of urgent correspondence and a painful personnel crisis on our staff.

The old me started to build up a head of steam to handle it all. While that steam often gets a lot done, it squeezes out of me joyful efficiency, and offers me a defensive spirit. I become a man all used up by the time he gets home. Just when peace was about to take a ride, and the air around me was becoming pressurized, my life support system once again pumped out better air— "The battle is not yours, but God's" (2 Chron. 20:15). Amazingly, I was able to relax as He opened up the best solutions to the stress-points.

The words of Jesus were giving me perspective.

Over and over that life-support system has sustained me.

As I planted Scripture deep in my personality, I was developing a powerful weapon for personal peace. No longer am I a slave to the tension in the atmosphere around me. I am breathing better air! It is taking concentration and discipline but stress is losing its grip on the steering wheel of my life.

Planting Season

These "victories for peace" were actually following a formula laid over three thousand years ago by King David. He shared his personal plan for staying on the main road:

I have hidden Your word in my heart, That I might not sin against You (Ps.119:11).

Jesus told His team that their fruitfulness—and ours—depends on "if...My words *remain* in you" (John 15:7). Many of His followers read the Bible, study the Bible, know the Bible...but most of us stop short of memorizing the Scriptures and counting on the Holy Spirit to make it part of our personalities.

And look—we don't have to run somewhere else to grab our life-support systems every time the air gets charged. It is with us at all times! We never know when we will be surprised by an unexpected temptation, a last straw, frustration, a turn for the worse. If we have been training our minds with scriptures, the pressure itself will help push His words into our conscious thinking. By reprogramming your personality you can reprogram your responses to pressure.

I found a simple plan to get "planting season" started. Aim to learn one verse each week. Once you see a verse that looks like good seed, you follow four planting procedures.

First, *theme it.*

It helps to have a category for the verse—a handle that helps pull it up when it's needed. Whether it is "prayer," "worry," "temptation," or "servanthood," learn the handle with the Scripture.

Second, *share it.*

Our family is "planting" together. If togetherness can

help Weight Watchers lose weight, then it can help Scripture Sowers, too. When Moses told the Jews to teach God's words to their children, he said:

"Fix these words of Mine in your hearts and minds" (Deut. 11:19).

That means this was meant to be something a family does together. Don't try to develop this discipline alone...buddy up!

Your third planting procedure is to *review it*.

Write it on a card and go over your verse as you drive or jog or shop or shower. I think that's a means of doing what the Bible calls "redeeming the time."

Of course, a good tool always helps when you're working on a project. We found a helpful Scripture planting tool...and we gave it to each other for Christmas. The Navigators have developed Scripture packets which they include in their Topical Memory System. The System can be ordered from NavPress, P.O. Box 6000, Colorado Springs, Colorado 80934. Since each packet contains twelve verses, organized by themes, you can have a review tool that offers concrete help.

The fourth step in planting Scripture is to *use it*.

What you do not use, you lose. We try to look for a real life place where we can plug in what we have planted. Recently our pastor spoke about the dependability of God's Word. After the service as the kids and I walked to our car, I combined all four procedures to review a verse we had just learned. We used the *theme* when I asked, "What verse about *the Word* tells us that God wrote it?" The *sharing* came as we said it together—thus *reviewing* it. And we had *used* it to enrich a sermon we had just heard.

The Shalom Factor

When a Jew speaks the ancient Hebrew greeting, "*Shalom*," he is using God's word for peace. *Shalom* is used over 250 times in the Old Testament where peace is the subject. It conveys much more than peace in the midst of a tranquil setting.

The biblical concept of peace, as communicated in *shalom*, is wholeness. If a person is complete and sound, then he has the Shalom Factor. Circumstances are secondary. Commenting on the meaning of peace in the Bible, one leading reference work says: "Peace means more than mere absence of war. Implicit in *shalom* is the idea of unimpaired relationships with others and fulfillment in one's undertakings."

In other words, if we have peace in ourselves and in our important relationships, the war won't get us down! The Shalom Factor outlasts the attack.

An Israeli soldier can smile and say, "*Shalom,*" even with a battle raging around him. If his orders, his squad, his weapons are set, then he has *shalom*. In the Hebrew understanding, it's when personal inner life or community life is out of order, that there is no peace.

Frankly, this is where my life had lost the Shalom Factor. I tended to blame my tensions on the latest crisis surrounding me. If we have to eliminate crises to get peace, then we're doomed to be a slave to stress. But remember stress has little to do with external pressure. It comes from internal disorder.

I had to "set my house in order." We are told to do that as preparation for dying...I needed it to prepare to *live*. Peace, by God's definition, is *restoring order*.

I knew that meant reorganizing my life around the quiet centers that make me a whole person. Wholeness begins when I launch my day by *Practicing the Presence of Christ*. I keep my perspective by insisting on REGULAR REST AND RECOVERY. Lovedness and interpersonal peace are guarded in that HUDDLE TIME WITH MY LIFE PARTNER. The stability of my inner circle is protected by CONSISTENT FAMILY FAITH TIMES. And Scripture planted in me enables me to REPROGRAM MY PERSONALITY with peaceful responses.

When our quiet centers become optional, stress takes charge again. They are easily compromised, steadily eroded...unless we stubbornly protect them.

Even at this first step on the pathway to personal peace, it is easy to see why the Bible calls it a pursuit. Quiet centers don't come naturally in our high-decibel lives. They have to be carved out at all cost, no matter what has to go to make room for them. Then they have to be protected daily against the encroachments that try to reclaim that sacred time.

The reward is personal "shalom"—a deep sense of wholeness that can handle the pressure. The alternative is constant turbulence and eventual collapse. Without the peace that comes from those quiet centers, we are like a house built near a storm-battered ocean beach. The beach keeps getting smaller and smaller until one storm finishes off the house.

Most of us have less "beach" left than we know. Quiet centers build a wall against the sea.

They restore order to our out-of-order lives.

Life's Gyroscopes

A gyroscope is basically a spinning wheel mounted in a movable frame. Amazing tricks are possible with this little gadget.

It can balance at an angle on the end of your finger even when you move your hand around. It can balance on the edge of a drinking glass and it will not fall even after a gentle nudge. If you point the axle of a rapidly spinning gyroscope at the sun, the end of the axle will appear to follow the sun as it crosses the sky. Amazingly, a gyroscope holds its original position in space while the earth turns under it.

When I was a kid, I thought a gyroscope was a toy. Actually, it is much more. The flight of that big 747 overhead is kept on course by the gyroscopes running the automatic pilot. The huge ocean liner steaming toward the Bahamas depends on its gyroscope to make sure it doesn't end up in Cuba. As the ship rolls back and forth in the sea, that little stabilizer is unaffected. No matter which way the ship is pointing, the gyroscope always points in the same direction.

There is something "gyroscopic" about the quiet centers

in our lives. If they are protected, we can balance on the edge, hold our original positions, always point in the same direction. The rolling surf and magnetic pulls cannot pull us off course.

Deep inner peace depends on maintaining five quiet centers. Peace is not passive. A gyroscope does not stand still. It may revolve 35,000 times a minute... always in motion. The quiet centers of personal peace are not puffy little clouds of contemplation that just float through our mental sky. If they are to stabilize our spinning life, they must *always be in motion*—kept at full speed by our aggressive attention.

We do not try to fit them into our busy lives. On the contrary, we establish our quiet centers and fit our busy lives around them! When we start to unravel again, we check to see which gyroscope has been left unguarded.

The downward pull of the earth's gravity does not affect a gyroscope in motion. If our quiet centers are intact, we can live in gyroscopic balance.

The downward pull has prevailed long enough. Our quiet centers give peace a chance.

Part III
Removing the Five Roots of Restlessness

8

Reaching for More

My wife's green thumb really lights up our yard. The geraniums, the dahlias, the roses are glorious. But not the poison ivy.

Of course, Karen did not plant the poison ivy. She discovered it by the front walk as she went to plant another rosebush. After fourteen scratch-free years, that ugly ivy was making a sudden appearance in our yard.

Apparently, it would be an easy thing to remove. After wrapping her hand and arm in a glove and a garbage bag, Karen tugged at the toxic weed. She was careful to pull up roots as well as plant. Or so she thought. About a month later another unwelcome three-leafer sprang up on the other side of the walk. Again, lawn surgery.

In spite of her efforts, the score is currently: Ivy 5, Karen 0. Following the same line across our yard, the poison ivy has been reincarnated five times! We keep pulling up the plants, but bits of the roots remain, only to poison our yard again another day.

Personal peace, like roses and geraniums, must be constantly planted, cultivated, and weeded. I am just beginning to see my peace-blossoms in a new joy for living, loving, working, listening. My schedule is still heavy, but it doesn't weigh nearly as much as it used to. This peace I have been pursuing is planted and being secured in those quiet centers

I am learning to protect.

But the poison ivy of stress still grows in my brightening yard. I'm finding that I must do more than pull up the unwelcome plant. The pursuit of peace demands I aggressively keep on removing the *roots* of stress! And honestly, they go deeper than I ever imagined.

The stress weeds are quite easy to see—overcrowded schedules, children's cries, academic pressures, chronic financial crunches, endless lists, relentless phone calls, stubborn people, and strained relationships. It is tempting to see these as the problem, but they're not. They are only symptoms of what's troubling us.

There is little point in giving a man with a brain tumor just two aspirin for his headache. He needs to have the cancer treated, not just the discomfort. In a similar way, if stress is seen only as a "too-busy" headache, it will never be significantly reduced.

Stress must be attacked at its *source*. Beneath the wear and tear of our lives—the poison ivy plants—is a chronic restlessness. Any plan to slow down our personal rat race must deal with the demons that drive us... *the roots of restlessness*.

My personal liberation began with the realization that pursuing peace is a battle with two fronts. I must be mobilized to *insist* on those quiet centers of peace, and to *resist* stress at its roots. If I am tired of being driven, then I have to face what's driving me!

The Appetite That's Never Satisfied

Commercials play to our restlessness, and they even help to create it. If they succeed, we feel a need for their product by the time their pitch is over. We want better breath, smoother hands, a nicer smell, or a bigger burger.

One potato chip commercial shows a boy boarding a bus with a big bag of their crunchies. As the boy keeps reaching for another chip, he claims, "Bet you can't eat just one." Hearing the irresistible crunch, the bus driver grabs "just one." Of course, he keeps munching, until finally his hat is full of those habit-forming chips. By the end of the ad, every-one on the bus is chomping and singing, "You can't eat just one." That's amazing, when you consider you can't even get two people to speak to each other on the buses I ride!

But the advertisers are experts on human motivation. They want to create in us *the appetite for more*. Even without those commercials, we are driven by that appetite.

"More" is usually perceived as the answer to our restless-ness, the "if-only-I-had's" of life. We convince ourselves that there's nothing wrong with us that wouldn't be cured by more time, more house, more money, more friends, more job, more clothes, more excitement, more comforts.

Then we get the "two aspirin" form of a big raise, a dream home, a partner, a lighter schedule or a standing ova-tion—only to find that the "headache" of restlessness soon returns.

The unsettling truth is that *more is never enough*! Discontent-ment destroys any possibility of personal peace. It condemns us to the pressure cooker of guaranteed restlessness.

Conventional wisdom tells us, "A man's reach should al-ways exceed his grasp." A commitment to excellence, to service, to personal purity should keep us reaching. We are, by nature, pursuers. That's why God calls us to pursue peace! But much modern stress results from the wrong pur-suits, misplaced discontentment.

We are enslaved by expectations which cannot be satis-fied. They are intrinsically frustrating. These "drivers" come in three forms, and they keep us on edge because they keep us reaching for more.

1. *Possession Expectations*

Plato commented insightfully on our possession expecta-tions:

"Poverty consists not in the decrease of one's possessions but in the in-crease of one's greed."

There is always another "thing" you don't have! And the increase of things only creates an appetite for more. There was a time we looked forward to owning one TV, but then we needed two. Once we were thrilled with an apartment of our own, but the thrill was soon replaced with a hankering for a little house of our own. Eventually the little house was too little. It would take a big house to do the trick. And a swimming pool would be nice, too.

Our "poverty" really is, in Plato's words, "the increase of one's greed." Dinner out at McDonald's was a once-special treat—now it's routine. Tonight it will take a fancy restaurant to provide the same special treat. It seems only yesterday that an air conditioner was the luxury of the rich—today I've got to have one. Yesterday's luxury has become today's necessity.

Life's goodies are truly good when God provides them in His way, in His time. They are enslaving when we demand them...when we expect them. Possession expectations will keep pushing us past the fragile limits of peace.

2. *People expectations*

We live in a state of chronic frustration because the significant others in our lives don't measure up. Or can't measure up.

Author James Dobson points out that while the baby is on the way, we profess only to want a child who is normal. But from birth on, we want a superkid! We want for him either the life we didn't have or a replay of the life we did have. Somehow, their grades, their friends, their style are never good enough. We focus on what they need to improve, seldom on what they have achieved.

So our children are quickly caught up with us in the whirlpool of more.

Marriages become battlefields because our partners continually disappoint us. Weaknesses are magnified; strengths are forgotten—just the reverse of the courtship process. We are expecting more of Prince Charming or Cinderella, and they may be getting tired of never being enough.

These people expectations can make a person incurably restless with his work. No working conditions, no boss is what you really wanted. And the dissatisfaction syndrome can reach right into the church, too. There is ultimately something wrong with every pastor, every leader. We end up expecting of people around us a perfection that belongs only to God.

If you are not satisfied with those around you, you are probably even less satisfied with yourself. We compare ourselves to standards of parenting, partnering, or producing that are unattainable, and can never relax because we are never good enough.

Marsha grabbed me after church one day to pour out her broken heart over her prodigal son. She had tried so hard and done everything she could, and he was walking on the wild side of life. As we talked, it became evident that Marsha had an unreasonably high standard for her son, one he could never quite hit. I suggested to her that a child who is never good enough may one day stop trying to be. He may choose a rebellious course that will remove any possibility of impossible expectations. Her son had opted out of the demands, only to create a whole new arena of pressure.

Marsha began to cry as she revealed the reason she had pushed her son so hard. She had grown up in the brokenness left by an alcoholic father. Her youthful agony made her resolve to be a perfect mother, to have a perfect home. She had walked that tightrope for years, and her son's struggles always threatened her goals. If he wasn't good enough, then *she* wasn't good enough. She was always reaching for more from him, from herself. Neither of them could find peace.

If our hopes for peace are placed in the hands of imperfect people, they are bound to evaporate.

3. *Performance expectations*

Performance drives us to stressful schedules, sacrifices, and compromises. Our worth becomes identified with our work, and no spot on the mountain is ever enough. Even the top is unsatisfying, as Alexander the Great discovered when he wept because there were no more worlds to conquer.

Amy started high school with the futility of performance

expectations. She seemed sad most of the time, so sad that she found herself on the brink of suicide. Although she outgrew those depths of depression, she did not grow much of a smile. The irony of her personal dissatisfaction was that she was a high achiever! She was elected vice-president of her school chorus, but she was miserable because she was not president. She ranked second in her class academically, but she chose to look at the one student ahead of her rather than the three hundred behind her. The storm in Amy seldom abated because winning was her only option.

Whatever our game is, we will lose consistently if we have to win. We aspire to be promoted to the next rung on the company ladder—only to need yet the next promotion before the paint is dry on our new office door. No award, no achievement is ever enough. We punish our bodies, our families, our friends, our sanity to reach for another level of victory.

One day this unquenchable appetite for conquest can even violate the marriage covenant. There is the "need" to demonstrate that you are still attractive. The innocent flirtations are tantalizing...you, your spouse, your kids—and even your conquest—end up sacrificed on the ugly altar of adultery.

It is stress-driven slavery always to have *something to prove*.

Discontentment runs like a treadmill under our feet. We are always running, pushing for more possessions, more from people, more conquest. There is no rest on a treadmill. Discontentment is the mortal enemy of peace...a deep root of stress and restlessness.

The Theory of "Relativity"

I think I'm short. For a 5'8" American male, "short" seems to be the verdict. However, I got a different perspective when I went to Singapore on teaching assignment. For one whole week, I was *tall*. And I am tall next to my youngest son, Brad, although that measurement is subject to change.

"Short," like so many other self-perceptions, is a matter of *comparison*. And *comparison is where discontentment begins*.

One of the battle cries around our house is, "How come Lisa...?" Since our eldest is, by age, the leader of the pack, her privileges become the standard of comparison for her two younger brothers. A situation that might otherwise be acceptable is suddenly "unfair" because of a look at Lisa. In those moments, two boys have based their contentment on a totally relative standard.

Simon Peter did it when Jesus was giving him his future assignments. Peter pointed to John and said, "Lord, what about *him*?" (John 21:21).

Jesus seemed to say, "Don't compare My plans for you with anyone else's." "If I want him to remain alive until I return, what is that to you? You must follow *Me*" (John 21:22).

The Old Testament Jews lived looking around, too. They were ruled by God through the wise judge, Samuel, but all the other nations around them had *kings*. Even though they were at peace and their enemies were defeated, they were restless. Samuel warned them that a king would draft their children as servants, build an empire that would be fueled with their funds and their families, and interfere constantly in their lives.

But the people refused to listen to Samuel. "No!" they said. "We want a king over us. Then we will be *like all the other nations*, with a king to lead us..." When Samuel heard all that the people said, he repeated it before the LORD. The LORD answered, "Listen to them and give them a king" (1 Sam. 8:19-22).

By insisting on a king, the Jews traded peace for stress. God gave them what they coveted, and they paid for it— along with generations of their descendants. It is no wonder that Paul warned: "When they measure themselves by themselves and compare themselves with themselves, they are not wise" (2 Cor. 10:12).

Of course, we always seem to compare ourselves to someone better off than we are. My eyes only see those whom I perceive to be more wealthy, more attractive, more talented, more comfortable, more privileged. And their "More" becomes the source of my next complaint, my next expectation.

My recent trip to Haiti provided an all-too-brief break from the cycle. I lived those few days among people who are lucky to have one small meal every other day, who draw their water from polluted trenches, and who die very young in a no-exit poverty. Suddenly, I was on the winning end by comparison, embarrassed by how much I have. I realized that the poorest American is probably richer than most of the world.

To live "looking around" is to feel forever like a loser.

Discontentment is a pirate that plunders personal peace. It pushes us beyond peaceful boundaries for our life.

That's what happened to Dave and Lois. After their first months in a ministry career, they started comparing themselves—not with other people who were new in the ministry, but with the affluent families in their area. Their rental home was not enough. Lois needed a home of her own. Against all outside advice and Dave's own misgivings, they stretched their economic systems to accommodate a mortgage. Over the years, that reach produced a long list of pressurized choices.

Lois had to work, even with a child at home to raise. Dave had to moonlight to pay for contingencies they had neglected in figuring for a mortgage. A spiral of debt caused friction, distance, even physical difficulties. Discontentment had trapped a young family in the vise grip of stress.

That appetite for more is always pushing—Mom out to work when the kids need her...people past their income budget...a husband or wife past their partner, an indebted Dad into a second job, the ladder climber to make unacceptable sacrifices to get to the next rung. And breakable children must live under crushing adult pressures.

Like an octopus, the tentacles of overcommitment constrict us. That reach for more finally leaves us with far less than we started with!

The "peace pirate" of discontentment also *robs us of the enjoyment of what we already have*. One of the pleasant assignments of a Jesus-follower is to be a wholehearted enjoyer! The Scriptures happily announce that God "richly provides us with *everything for our enjoyment*" (1 Tim. 6:17).

My son cannot really enjoy the Christmas gift he just opened if he is more interested in what his brother got—and how it compares. We miss the talents, the opportunities, the good things we *have* because we are focused on what we *do not have*.

Contentment does not consist of getting everything you always wanted to have. It is realizing *how much you already have*.

Discontentment also diminishes us because it denies the goodness of God. It hurts me, as the provider for our family, if my children complain they do not have the clothes, the books, the food they need. Ultimately, our grumbling, audible or implied, attacks the adequacy of God's fathering of His kids! We are, in essence, saying, "The Lord is my Shepherd, but I still want."

The roots of restlessness are thus fiercely connected to our reaching for more. Discontentment drives us to a life of hurt and pressure. The biblical equation states:

Godliness with contentment is great gain. For we brought nothing into the world, and we can take nothing out of it. But if we have food and clothing, we will be content with that (1 Tim. 6:6-8).

The human nature equation says that great gain is the result of reaching. God says it comes from resting. Contentment is not laziness, not for a minute! It frees me to pursue aggressively what is worth pursuing, things that satisfy deep down.

The contentment equation is followed by a description of the great loss of restless reaching:

People who want to get rich [more!] fall into temptation and a trap and
into many foolish and harmful desires that plunge men into ruin and
destruction. For the love of money is a root of all kinds of evil. Some
people, eager for money, have wandered from the faith and pierced
themselves with many griefs (1 Tim. 6:9-10).

The language is strong. The discontentment lifestyle leads
to "a trap," to "foolish and harmful desires," to "ruin and
destruction," to being "pierced" with "many griefs."

The appetite for more always leaves people hungry, if not
poisoned.

Learning to Rest

"Be content with what you have" (Heb. 13:5). That is the
simple biblical alternative to the reach for more. If we can
learn contentment, we finally "seek peace."

The call to the higher ground of contentment embraces
three of life's great arenas. The "be content" verse opens
with contentment with your material position:

"Keep your lives free from the love of money" (Heb.
13:5).

Jesus pointed to the well-fed birds and the well-dressed
lilies to show what kind of a Provider God is. With that back-
drop, He talked about two pursuits, one worthless, the other
worthwhile:

"Do not set your heart on what you will eat or drink; do not worry about it.
For the pagan world runs after all such things, and your Father knows
that you need them. *But seek His kingdom*, and these things will be given
to you as well" (Luke 12:29-31).

The material position of God's child is not the result of
trying to "seek after" such things. That is the preoccupation
of the "nations of the world" who are orphans on their own.
Our Father "knows that you need these things." Our Father
is looking after what we need so we can seek what He values.
We can drop out of the rat race for more because our Father
guarantees we will always have *enough*. He frees our hands to
fix broken relationships, help the helpless, love our family,

introduce people to Christ—the real concerns of His kingdom.

Enough is all we need, and enough is guaranteed. The things most people are trying to take "will be given to you." C. S. Lewis wisely summed it up:

Aim at heaven and you will get earth thrown in;
aim at earth and you will get neither.

Contentment begins when you relax with your material position.

Water From Your Own Cistern

There's a haunting ballad that describes a "restless wind that yearns to wander." That restless wind blows through many marriages today. Long before it is consciously admitted, there is a smoldering urge to see if there is "greener grass."

There isn't.

When the Bible says, "Be content with what you have" (Heb. 13:5), it precedes that call with strong words. "Marriage should be honored by all, and the marriage bed kept pure, for God will judge the adulterer and all the sexually immoral" (Heb. 13:4).

God's reference to "contentment" here is to contentment with our marriage partners. That seems to have little to do with the partner's condition. It has mostly to do with our personal commitment.

Drink water from your own cistern,
Running water from your own well.
Should your springs overflow in the streets, your
streams of water in the public squares?
Let them be yours alone, never to be shared with strangers...
and may you rejoice in the wife of your youth...
...may her breasts satisfy you always,
may you ever be captivated by her love (Prov. 5:15-19).

The Bible clearly commands us to find all our sexual fulfillment, all our sexual enjoyment in one person. It is a daily decision a married person makes to say, "My mate is more than enough." As soon as fantasies start to divide our attention, we begin to lose the intensity of the physical relationship. But when our life partner is the total focus of our affection, we will be "captivated" and "satisfied" once again.

As for drinking from a cistern other than your own, "The evil deeds of a wicked man ensnare him; the cords of his sin hold him fast" (Prov. 5:22).

Marital restlessness is deadly business. Marital contentment is life-giving.

Discovering the Day He Made

Those first few minutes in the bathroom each morning can really be depressing. I look in the mirror, constantly amazed by how much damage one night's sleep can do. The tools of reconstruction are activated—washcloth, toothbrush, comb, razor. Usually the improvement is only modest, just a little better than the disaster I started with.

My wife must have known I would need a lift in those semicomatose moments. She put up a little plaque just beneath the bathroom mirror. It reminds me every morning:

This is the day the LORD has made; let us rejoice and be glad in it (Ps. 118:24).

I need to remember, early enough, that I don't goof up, that I am not *designing* a day but *discovering* a day He has already made. That makes it an OK day even before I see what's in it.

I think that means I am learning the other dimension of a relaxed spirit—*contentment with your life position*. Locked in a dingy prison cell, Paul chose to be a victor rather than a victim when he wrote:

I have learned to be content whatever the circumstances...I have learned the secret of being *content in any and every situation*, whether well fed or hungry, whether living in plenty or in want. I can do everything through Him who gives me strength (Phil. 4:11-13).

It is no accident that Paul had just finished writing about "the peace of God, which transcends all understanding" (Phil. 4:7). Personal peace is inextricably tied to contentment in "any and every situation."

This "it's-OK" spirit belongs to the person who knows that today is not the creation of your friends, your enemies, your boss, your family, your luck. Rather, the Lord has made each day in such a way that just the right people will be in just the right place at just the right time.

Because I am a planner by nature, I really wrestle with contentment in the apparent detours of life. I hate Murphy's Law about things going wrong, and I often revert to stressful responses when Murphy wins.

But the pursuit of peace is teaching me something about God's playing fields in my life. My plans may call for a wide field with plenty of money, good health, and smooth sailing. Then, for reasons I will understand later, God pulls in the boundaries. A sick wife, the loss of a job—or a promotion—a child with a broken arm, a financial setback, car trouble, disturbed relationships, a closed door. These "circumstances beyond our control" give us less running room.

We can try to keep running at the same speed, fighting the Lord's plans. Or we can adjust our speed and know His peace.

To be content with our life position cancels out the reach for more. It means that *who* we are is OK—our looks, our abilities, our singleness. *Where* we are is OK, too—our address, our school, our job, our position. And contentment includes *how* you are, even in a sickbed or with an empty wallet.

Contentment does not mean we do not work and pray for a change—that's why you "present your requests to God" (Phil. 4:13). It does mean resting in His plans and His timing while working toward a change.

When contentment begins to invade those three life arenas—material possessions, marriage partner, and life position—it brings joyous new freedom. Like a child who expects his father to take care of everything, we will once again taste the innocence of trust and peace.

The Weapons of Contentment

The "contenter" has a pressure problem. Our entire environment pushes us on to compare, complain, compete, and conquer. In order to develop equal pressure on the inside, we need to know how to use the weapons of contentment: a secure Source, a grateful memory, and a realistic reach.

First, we need to renew our daily confidence in our secure Source. When something happens to our paycheck, our breadwinner, or our best friend, we feel a deep sense of fear and restlessness. But those are only vehicles of God's supply, not the Source. He is infinitely creative in finding other ways to send what we need. After all, our Father is the inventor of manna in the wilderness, water from a rock, and food delivered free by ravens.

If we are God's because we chose Christ, then our Source is beyond the reach of any recession, depression, or hydrogen bomb.

Second, we fight discontentment with *a grateful memory*. King David "talked to himself" on a very high level when he said: "Be at rest once more, O my soul,/For the LORD has been good to you" (Ps. 116:7). David had known about "soul rest" for a long time. He had put it into practice on the distinctly *un*restful occasion of facing Goliath. His memory was working well when he challenged the giant with these words: "The LORD who delivered me from the paw of the lion and the paw of the bear will deliver me from the hand of this Philistine" (1 Sam. 17:37).

On the days when the giants "shiver our timbers," it helps to remember how God handled the lions and bears we have faced before. If our thank-you lists are up to date, we find a confident contentment.

Several weeks ago I was impressed with the importance of gratitude when Brad, our youngest, gave me a handmade Father's Day gift. I said, "If you can wait just a few minutes, then I can take time to appreciate what you made."

He caught me by surprise when he said, "Oh, not like with the candle holder, huh?"

I was baffled until he reminded me of another handmade gift he had given me several months before. I was on the run, gave it a passing glance, and broke his heart. I had not realized how insensitive I had been, or how much an unappreciated gift wounds the giver.

God knows how Brad felt. He sends His gifts to us daily, but we are too busy to notice or to say thanks. As a result, we lack the poise that comes from being in touch with God's goodness. Regular, specific thanks warm our Father's heart, and reconfirm our contentment in a restless moment. If He's done it before, He will do it again!

The third weapon of contentment is *a realistic reach*. Before you set a goal, you candidly assess the time, the talents, and the resources you have. Jesus rebuked those who started a tower without calculating what it would take to finish it (see Luke 14:28-30). The crash can be prevented by checking your fuel tanks first!

Again, King David revealed another secret of a relaxed spirit, "My heart is not proud, O Lord, my eyes are not haughty;/I do not concern myself with great matters or things too wonderful for me./But I have stilled and quieted my soul" (Ps. 131:1-2).

We must know our strengths, and limitations. Our lives were meant to be built on that list of all the capabilities and personality strengths a good God has given us. We do not need to waste time living in our limitations.

If we decide to do a few things well, we will avoid the curse of overcommitment. There is great satisfaction in focused energy and completed towers. If your reach will compromise a quiet center or pushes you beyond the boundaries of peace, consider it too expensive. King Solomon had his values straight when he counseled:

Better one handful with tranquillity than two handfuls with toil and
chasing after the wind (Eccles. 4:6).

A classic moment in the *Pogo* comic strip portrays Pogo
and company following the footprints of their enemy. Everyone has been so engrossed in tracking this elusive foe that no
one has noticed where the path has led. Finally, when Pogo
realizes the footprints have led them in a circle, it dawns on
him that these are their own footprints. Pogo observes in unforgettable fashion—"We have found the enemy...and he is
us!"

In our battle to track and defeat stress, it is easy to pursue
the wrong enemy. It appears to us that the enemies are *without*—family members, deadlines, co-workers, school,
friends, phones, bills. In reality, many of those life-twisters
are there because of the real enemies *within*!

When we are willing to recognize that the enemy is us,
stress can be beaten. When we see the pressure *we create for
ourselves* because of our appetite for more, then peace is
within reach.

We have found a powerful root of the restlessness in our
heart. We can dig up discontentment by its roots—and plant
rosebushes where poison ivy has been.

9

Revolving around Ourselves

I was in the "five-minutes-before-closing" line at the bank when a lady came bustling in. She stood behind me, muttering all the while about her overstuffed day. As she fumbled to prepare her deposit, my flustered neighbor sighed and exclaimed, "Somebody's got to slow this world down!"

"Or," I ventured, "we're going to have to learn to slow down in this world."

The dear lady is far from being alone in her whirlwind. As I have told my determination to "seek peace, and pursue it," people respond in deeply personal ways. When I discussed it on radio, the mail exploded with letters from fellow stress addicts. When I shared the early chapters of this book with a group of editors, they said after reading them, "How could you know so much about us?" After only two chapters were completed, the wife of a busy executive grabbed my hand and said, "How soon can you finish this? You've written about me!"

What began for me as a very personal search has shown me how peace poor all of us are! As I introduce the idea of a peace alternative, my friends get a look in their eyes that is part hope, part skepticism. It is as if they are saying, "I'm tired of being a two-legged tornado. But is it possible to live any other way?" Like people with a disease, they urgently

hope for a cure that works. And those who know me are confident, "If it can work for him, it could work for anybody!"

Personal peace is expensive. But, compared to strangula-
tion by stress, it's a bargain! Peace requires both a stubborn
commitment to quiet centers and a painful honesty about the
roots of our restlessness. Pulling up those poisonous roots of
stress reaches into the most personal corners of our lives.
Like exploring a long-neglected basement, our light reveals
messes we have ignored for a long time. But if we are desperate enough for change, we won't run from the realities.

The Great Big Me

Self-centeredness is "doing what comes naturally." Before
a child can walk or talk, he learns to get his world revolving
around him. He expects everything to stop when he wants to
be fed or burped or changed. For being such a "helpless little
thing," he surely can inflict a lot of misery on people who
don't come when he calls.

As that little baby grows, the magic word appears early:
"Mine!" Most of his conflicts center around that word.

The babies inside us are still alive and well. Our needs are
much greater, our cries more sophisticated. But we may still
be in the business of trying to keep life revolving around us.
In so doing, we create personal isolation and dissatisfaction
that keep stress thriving.

When Steve was in high school, he created an impressive
orbit around himself. He was one of the top-ranked football
players in his city, tops in his class academically, and going
steady with the outstanding senior girl.

Steve asked to talk to me one day. As we walked around
the football field for the third time, he stopped and looked at
the ground, as if he were looking for the words he needed.
Finally, Steve blurted, "I'm lonely."

I expressed surprise in light of his enviable popularity in
school.

"Sure, everything's going my way," he explained. "I have
hit every goal I aimed for. I've made my world everything I

could make it. But *a world that's only as big as I am is just too small to live in."*

"Too small to live in" is the ultimate measurement of any life that revolves around self. Unfortunately many of us do not learn that truth at seventeen as Steve did. Our push for "mine" creates anxiety and pressure all around us, and all in us. We are incurably restless until we get ourselves out of the middle.

My dictionary lists *192* words that are "self-" compound words. That, in itself, should tell us something. The list includes many ways to get life revolving around me. I have selected the "Big Four."

The Crusader... Self-fulfillment

"Grab a sign and march!" That seems to be the battle cry again in our day as a thousand diverse groups demand their "rights." One political observer noted that a modern Presidential candidate must be conscious of fifty different "rights" groups, each of which represents 2 percent of the population. Our society is fragmented by a cacophony of voices screaming "Mine!"

Out of the seventies—"the Me Decade"—came a militant "mineness." Beyond the societal marching, a deeply personal demand for self-fulfillment arose. Husbands, wives, parents, children, friends marching for self-fulfillment as individuals. We have caught the contagion of discontentment with whatever, whoever we are.

If we listen carefully, we may hear the "crusader's" sentiments in our own hearts, in sentences such as:

- "Now it's finally time for *me.*"
- "After all I've sacrificed, I have this *coming.*"
- "I *deserve* this."
- "I have to look out for *myself* for a change."
- "I have a *right* to this."

Decisions tend to be made on the basis of the "entitled to's." In reality, our entitlements are just good, old-fashioned selfishness in a stylish modern disguise. We have actually managed to make self-centeredness seem noble.

The truth is that I find *my* happiness by seeking yours . . . but the lie has prevailed. That lie shouts, "I will only find fulfillment if I pursue my own happiness." There may be a lot of wreckage around us before we realize that self-happiness always runs faster than we do!

I had just finished speaking on peace at a local church when a woman asked to talk with me. She was well-dressed, attractive, but in tears. She told about how she responded to the siren song of career fulfillment, neglecting her family in the process. Now her life was filled with the stresses of success in work and failure at home.

"I can't believe I fell for it!" She told me, "We women have watched the price our men have paid for chasing success—the heart attacks, the pressure, the broken relationships. And now we have followed them right down that same rat hole! We're as stressed out as they are!"

A woman may have to work to balance the budget, but not to find her identity. The marching orders for Mom have not changed:

Train the younger women to love their husbands and children, to be self-controlled and pure, to be busy at home, to be kind, and to be subject to their husbands, so that no one will malign the word of God (Titus 2:4-5).

A man who falls for the self-fulfillment marching song will see his office as his major life arena, not his home. He may consider it a fair trade to succeed in his career at the expense of failing in his family. If anything his family will be treated as mere accessories.

Whether we lose ourselves in a career, church work, or an "affair," the self-fulfillment obsession will diminish a life, not enhance it. Insisting on "my rights," "my way" is the beginning of the end of peace.

Living is giving, and the self-fulfillment crusade makes us

live "on the take." No matter how many "rights" we get, we will be too alone to be fulfilled.

The Crusher...Self-Absorption

Someone once observed: "I just met a man who was all wrapped up in himself. Sure was a small package!" Although a self-absorbed person may be a "small package," he can raise the misery index in lives all around him.

And the busier we get, the more self-absorbed we are. We are so preoccupied with our responsibilities, our fatigue, our unfinished work that we can't seem to fit anyone else in! When life overheats, children become intruders, coworkers are a nuisance, and every other driver is in our way.

We get caught in a vicious cycle: stress makes us selfish— then selfishness makes us stressful. For a while everyone may fall into orbit around our obsession. But eventually the whispers we were too preoccupied to hear will become cries that pierce our heart. The hurts we have inadvertently inflicted as we raced by will pile up at our doorstep. And we will find ourselves cut off from the very support system that makes us strong enough to handle stress. Self-absorbed living is a runaway bulldozer that crushes everyone and everything that gets in its way.

A "small package" person is not much fun to be around. No matter what folks were discussing, the conversation is about him, once he arrives. He dominates with how *he* feels, where *he* has been, how hard *he* is working, what *he* has planned.

He doesn't really hear when people speak. His mind is on his personal agenda. In the process, he misses many statements that will reappear later in more demanding form. And because he is wrapped up in himself, he tends to come home like a "spoiled king," expecting the family either to get out of his way or pamper him.

A self-absorbed "crusher" pushes people to the fringes of his life without even realizing it. His pursuits may be wholesome—until they become his central preoccupation. The telephone, the tennis game, the Bible studies, the workshop, the classes—life is filled with good things that can become "magnificent obsessions."

Self-absorption may have reduced your life to one that is only revolving around you. When I tried to see myself through the eyes of my wife, my children, my friends, my coworkers, I saw a man much too preoccupied for them to reach. Walking a mile in the shoes of those closest to me helped me to see a small package.

That crusher of self-centeredness will do a U-turn someday and crush us, too, unless we send it away before it does any more damage.

The Crippler...Self-Appointedness

In the "Peanuts" comic strip, Lucy has found a "helpful" way to get everyone revolving around her. She is everyone's problem solver. Lucy can be found at that converted lemonade stand, under a big sign that says, "Psychiatric help—5¢." The price may be right, but the advice leaves a little to be desired.

Real-life Lucys position themselves right in the middle of everything that needs to be done. They are always available, always helping hurting people, always giving, always doing the work. The problem is in that word *always*. They are essentially self-appointed sacrificers.

To be sure, self-sacrifice is a distinctly Christian virtue. Jesus' followers are called upon to "carry each other's burdens" (Gal. 6:2). In fact, if more Christians would copy Christ in giving of themselves, the spiritual "rescue squad" might not burn out so often. We should be the burden bearers, but not always.

There is, in the people-helping lifestyle, the danger of developing a "Messiah complex," you begin to *assume* the responsibility for the problems of every person around you...and for every unfinished task around. As noble as that might seem, this self-appointedness will hurt instead of help. If you self-sacrifice until there is no self left, the whole network tied to you will collapse when you do.

What begins as unselfish service can sometimes become a neurotic dependency between the helper and the "helpees." People are crippled if someone always comes when they call. Parents know that loving a child sometimes means being "unavailable," so the child can learn to handle it himself. If we always run to tie a child's shoe, fix a toy, or pack his lunch, he will grow up deprived of important life skills. In the same way, people grow up emotionally weak if "Lucy" appoints herself to be there every time they hurt.

Moses was practicing this self-appointed brand of serving as Israel's one and only judge in the wilderness. The courts were all backed up, waiting for Moses. Jethro, his father-in-law, gave the kind of advice that is still valid for those of us who tend toward a Messiah complex today.

When his father-in-law saw all that Moses was doing for the people, he said, "What is this you are doing for the people? Why do you alone sit as judge, while all these people stand around you from morning till evening?" Moses answered him, "Because the people come to me to seek God's will."...Moses' father-in-law replied, "*What you are doing is not good*. You and these people who come to you will only *wear yourselves out* [mutual burnout!]. The work is too heavy for you; *you cannot handle it alone*...select capable men from all the people....Have them serve as judges for the people...That will make your load lighter, because they will share it with you. If you do this...you will be *able to stand the strain*, and all these people will go home satisfied" (Exod. 18:14-15, 17, 21-23).

Everyone around the over-helper ends up frustrated— most of all, the helper himself. The well of his concern is never enough and it eventually dries up (or burns out) from unlimited use. If you try to do all the jobs and solve all the problems, you are condemned to a life of relentless stress and frustrated restlessness. And there goes peace. There is only one Messiah. He will carry the weight of people's burdens, and develop other leaders. We should always be ready to sacrifice when the Master prompts us to help meet someone's need—but *only* when He does.

The Complainer...Self-Pity

While we still have the newspaper open to the cartoons, we can take a look at another classic "Peanuts" character, Pigpen. He is the sort of kid to be let into the yard, but not into the house. One can always tell Pigpen is coming by the cloud of dust. Apparently, the little guy misplaced the bathtub and the dust of the ages falls whenever he moves.

I suppose we all know people who bring a cloud with them wherever they are. They have developed a way of getting things to revolve around them called *self-pity*. They carry a cloud of complaints that usually helps them at least get attention, if not get their way. It works for a time—until it backfires.

A "pity party" celebrates every physical ailment, every unfairness, every difficulty, every need. By compiling complaints, the self-pitier loses his perspective and labels himself one of life's victims.

Self-pity is particularly unbecoming in a parent or partner. The script has some recurring lines:

- "How could you *do* this to me?"
- "After all I've sacrificed for you."
- "Why can't you help when I'm in this condition?"

A child or a spouse can be manipulated with a guilt game like that—until he cracks up, blows up, or gives up.

No one needs more dark clouds in life. That is why people ultimately withdraw from the person who is preoccupied with his own problems. At that point, the self-pitier can either use that rejection as something else to pity...or face himself and the neurotic bondage he puts people in.

Like all the other "self" people, the self-pitier is always restless. He drives away the very attention he craves and actually looks for stress to complain about. Like Pigpen, he gets lost in his own cloud of dust.

The Stress of the Times

As I thumb through my *Newsweek*, I keep coming across words like *apocalypse* and *Armageddon*. These are Bible words, not *Newsweek* words. Their presence in reporters' vocabularies reflects a growing "last days" consciousness around the world.

Those last days are generally regarded as being dangerous times in which to live. According to the Bible, they will be—but for a surprising reason: "There will be terrible times in the last days" (2 Tim. 3:1).

That word translated "terrible" literally means in the original Greek "hard times" or "times of stress." The last days will be stress times, but not only because of armaments, antichrists, or earthquakes. The danger will be in what people have become:

People will be lovers of themselves (2 Tim. 3:2).

The ultimate stress this planet will ever know is a direct result of people revolving around themselves. The descriptive words that follow catalog the loss of everything of value in the human experience: "People will be...lovers of money, boastful, proud, abusive, disobedient to their parents, ungrateful, unholy, without love, unforgiving, slanderous, without self-control, brutal, not lovers of the good"(2 Tim. 3:2-3).

Self-love leads to life without love. When love becomes twisted like that, ours becomes a dangerous world. When the Bible adds up the sum of self-centered living, the total is sobering. When we live with life revolving around ourselves—whether through self-fulfillment, self-absorption, self-appointed sacrifice, or self-pity—we eventually *lose the ability to give or receive love*. That is a price too high to pay.

Our parrot loves to look at his own reflection. Put him by the mirror and he will try to get a kiss, a caress, a response from that reflection. But there is no satisfaction to be found just looking at yourself. Peace is not found in the mirror either. I am finding it in Jesus. His peace leaves me fully involved with others, but free inside. In fact, He proposes a radical lifestyle alternative to life's revolving around me. He challenges any *E Pluribus Me* attitude we may have with these startling words:

"Whoever wants to save his life will lose it, but whoever loses his life for me will save it" (Luke 9:24).

Hang onto our life, and we will lose it. Give it away, we will find it. The Prince of Peace prescribes *giving living*. Not only did He preach it, He lived it—even in the ugliest moment of His life. I know that even the mini-suffering of a twenty-four hour flu makes me self-centered. By contrast, during His ultimate suffering on the Cross, Jesus Christ still practiced giving living: "When Jesus saw His mother there, and the disciple whom He loved standing nearby, He said to His mother, 'Dear woman, here is your son,' and to the disciple, 'Here is your mother' " (John 19:27).

When we would fully expect Jesus to be thinking about his own agony, He was thinking about His family! What a blatant contradiction to the myth of "looking out for Number One."

Giving living is a source of strength in a stress-bombarded life. In his book, *You Can Profit from Stress*, Gary Collins documented how to find life by giving it away:

Based on studies of people under intense pressure, one psychologist concluded that those who survive longest seem to be those who expend most energy in helping and supporting others.

Seven Commitments Toward Peace

We can live with hands tightly clenched, protecting what is ours—and live in turmoil. Or, we can take the risk of living with open hands—and know God's special kind of peace. Let me suggest that giving living translates into everyday life through the following commitments:

1. *Live by the "what's best for everybody" principle.*

When I have a Sunday afternoon free, I like to go for a drive to the country. Since I work so-o-o hard all week, I figure I should call the shots for rec time. There have been times—before my pursuit of peace—when my desires overruled four other Hutchcrafts who wanted to stay home.

Now, however, I am listening more. We have discovered new levels of family fun since Dad tried doing "what's best for everybody." Dad has also learned, as a result, how to relax a little more on Sunday and run a little less. Whether it's deciding about time off, what to buy, what to eat, or family rules, yield to the "common good."

2. *Open your home.*

Overcrowded lives tend to breed a lifestyle of privatism. That means my home is my castle, and I raise the drawbridge when I'm home.

We have never lost, however, when we obey the biblical injunction to "practice hospitality" (Rom. 12:13).

Our family has been so enriched by those who have had "bed and breakfast" at our house. We have friends all over the world in whose lives we had a little investment...and they in ours. Giving living considers privatism as poverty. A home that is just for us is too small to live in.

3. *Focus on others when you arrive home (or when they arrive home).*

I always close my physical briefcase before I leave the office, but I sometimes leave my mental briefcase open long after I get home. In the same way, a homemaker deluged with laundry and leftovers coming and going can easily miss the people she loves most.

For me, the drive from the office is the time to focus on each family member. What was Karen's schedule? What tests did Brad have? If I've gotten in touch before I am with them, I can put them first when I walk in the door.

4. *Respond as a family to human needs.*

A grieving family, a husband out of work, a hospital stay, a financially pressed friend. These are golden moments to learn giving living. My wife's sensitive heart instinctively senses these opportunities and mobilizes our Care Brigade to do something about it. The day we scoured the house for toys and clothes we could give to inner-city kids without a Christmas is one of our warmest memories.

5. *Look for the person who needs you.*

The greatest cure for depression is finding someone to help. Giving living makes us look around our workplace, our friends, our home to ask, "Who needs me here?" It turns humdrum days into adventures.

6. *Take time for people.*

Our work is as temporary as last night's clean dishes or yesterday's memo. People are forever.

Keep that perspective when the day is too busy for a child or an interruption or a colleague. Explain why your time with him will be short, or set a later time to give him the attention he deserves. But don't ever let your list pre-empt your love.

7. *Be generous with your treasures.*

"One man gives freely, yet gains even more;/another withholds unduly, but comes to poverty./A generous man will prosper; *he who refreshes others will himself be refreshed* (Prov. 11:24-25).

Receiving is not the reason to give. But it is the result.

We had heard about a local ministry couple who were broke and had a serious case of Mother Hubbard's cupboards. Groceries were tight enough for us at that same time to give us pause as we put together a bag to take to our friends. No sooner had we returned home than the doorbell rang. A friend had felt led to bring us some groceries—*four* bags. I was a little embarrassed at having given so little, but very grateful.

Giving living asks, "Whose goods are these, anyway? Whose car? Whose money? Whose books or records?" We have concluded that they are His resources, given to us to manage. It's just a lot more fun to be *His* delivery boys than to be His warehouse!

General William Booth, the visionary founder of the Salvation Army, was very sick. His little mission to the poor of London had spread worldwide. His "soldiers" were meeting in an historic international convention, and General Booth was to deliver the keynote address. The sickness that kept him from coming would be his last.

The Salvationists longed for a message from their leader. From his deathbed General Booth dictated a one-word telegram, his last sermon. The General's final challenge carries a message across the years. His word: "Others!"

That word is a vibrant alternative to "mine." All our self-directed energies leave us empty, alone. A world that revolves around ourselves is a restless world, chasing fulfillment in places it can never be found.

"Others" living—*giving* living—is the peaceful new life we can plant where the root of self-seeking has been. And a heart tired from futile pursuits is finally free to pursue something better. Like peace...which always has an open hand.

10

Replaying Old Hurts

I found Carol sobbing on the dormitory steps. Her face was buried in her hands so all I could see was her close-cropped brown hair.

Carol and her husband Stan were in my classes. As I sat on the steps next to her, I heard her crying softly, "I'm no wife. I'm no wife at all."

After a borrowed handkerchief and a short walk, Carol explained: "Stan is such a good husband, but I never let him lead. I can't submit—to his decisions, to his spiritual leadership, or even sexually. I undermine him, no matter what he does. I'm destroying him!"

I noticed a dark look cross Carol's anguished face when she said, "Years ago I decided I would never let anyone else control my life." A little probing revealed that she was referring to her mother.

Any time Carol's mother could not get her way, she would freeze Carol out. She simply would not speak to her daughter again until Carol crawled back to her—physically, at times. Although she denied it at first, Carol hated her mother for that emotional abuse. Her marital problem was really a maternal problem. Unable to stand up to her mother, Carol defied Stan, an innocent surrogate.

We composed a letter together that day. Carol wrote, through hot tears, a letter to clear up her long-denied hate toward her mother and to propose a new, healthy mother-daughter relationship. We walked to the mailbox as if it were the corridor to "Death Row." With fear and trembling, Carol gambled on a new future with the decisive clunk of the mailbox lid.

Mom tried to freeze her out one last time. But Carol and Stan stood their ground. A new mother-daughter friendship was born through that pain. Most important, Carol was finally free to love Stan as she had wanted to for years. Their vibrant letters and confident children tell eloquently of the happiness they have found.

Carol needed more than medication or meditation for the stresses that tortured her. She needed to dig deep for a root of restlessness buried deep in her personality...for those old hurts she kept replaying on the screen of her heart.

The Bible directly connects peace with rooting out old bitternesses:

Make every effort to live in peace with all men.... See to it that no one misses the grace of God and that *no bitter root* grows up to cause trouble and defile many (Heb. 12:14-15).

Our peace is repeatedly sabotaged by bitterness. That which we have not forgiven surfaces in seemingly unrelated actions. When Carol hurt Stan, she never mentioned her mother. But the bitter feelings kept churning until the root was pulled up.

When our boys were little, we found twenty-two crazy things you could do with a beach ball. Often we would see how far beneath the water we could hold that ball. In the process, we learned a simple scientific principle: the farther down you push it, the higher it goes when you let go!

Each of us has emotional beach balls pushed down inside us. Perhaps these past scars do not enter our conscious mind very often. But bad feelings are not erased just because they are ignored or denied. Somewhere, sometime, they will go off—and "defile" many.

The source of the hurt may well be very real, very ugly. It

may have been verbal or physical abuse by a parent. The wounds can come from unfair treatment, devastating neglect, or shattered dreams. Whatever the cause, the resulting cancer of bitterness inflicts little damage on the "grudgee"— but it is killing to the grudger. You don't really hold a grudge. A grudge holds you.

When the police break up a riotous mob, they arrest and remove the agitators who are stirring up the troops. When the dignity of a trial is disrupted by an angry defendant or an emotional spectator, the judge bangs his gavel and insists, "Order in the court!" If the troublemaker persists, the bailiff will simply remove him from the courtroom. Disruption is best treated by evicting the instigator. That gets rid of the source of the disruption.

Disruption and disorder are the antithesis to the Christian experience of peace. That ancient Hebrew *shalom*, you will recall, is not the absence of war. It describes inner order, even amid conflict. The pursuit of personal peace, then, demands the eviction of whatever is causing the disorder inside, those bitter feelings that continually stir up trouble. For yesterday's wounds simply do not stay in yesterday. They creep into today, and tomorrow, with their poison.

Bitter Root, Bitter Fruit

We replay old hurts in three stress-producing ways. The first is in *distorted decisions*. The hurtee is in bondage to the hurter until forgiveness replaces the hurt. The presence of the hurter determines where to sit or not to sit, to go or not to go, to talk or not to talk. The thought of having to face that person is too much to handle. We are not free to move freely through our days. Our options are limited and our decisions distorted by the indirect influence of the person who has wounded us.

If, for example, a husband did the damage, the resulting wall twists every decision that involves him. If his wife wants to punish him, she cannot choose anything that will make him happy. If she wants to avoid him, she cannot choose anything that will bring him close. If she wants to pretend the hurt isn't there, she has to play her husband's game and keep conversation forever superficial.

It is the ultimate irony of bitterness that the people we would like to forget keep controlling our lives, looming larger than life. The old hurts distort our decisions by forcing us either to get even or get away.

The bitterness replays bring a second stressful effect in the form of *damaged self-worth*. A physical wound limits what the body can do; an emotional wound limits what the spirit can do.

Jeff just won't risk being loved, since the people he loved most broke his heart. Early in his junior high career, he set out to show his parents by his grades that they had the son they wanted. He worked feverishly, and proudly earned five A's and one B. It wasn't enough. Mom and Dad seemed interested only in Jeff's bringing that B up to an A. Some kids could have handled that unintended rebuff; Jeff was too sensitive.

Jeff's folks never knew the wound they had inflicted. In true macho fashion, their son kept it all inside. And it's still there in his senior year. He decided that he could never be good enough for people who loved him, that opening up to people can only lead to hurt. Jeff drinks too much, drives too fast, and recently attempted suicide. He needs people, but he can't let them get close. Wounded into believing he is a failure, he keeps replaying those feelings everywhere he goes.

Jeff has never told his parents about the hurt that has kept on hurting. And he has certainly never let go of the anger and disillusionment. Like many of us, he feels and acts as if he isn't important. And the roots of his restlessness are in a wound from years ago.

Harboring old hurts contributes to stress in a third way—*displaced dislike*. Anyone who reminds us of the hurter, whether rightly or wrongly, triggers the old feelings. That's why Carol was slowly destroying her husband. Even though he was an innocent party, his marital leadership brought back memories of those humiliating crawls to her mother.

If a father abuses a daughter, she may never let herself get close to a man. If a mother dominates a son, he may resist the help and strength of a woman throughout his life. Friends, bosses, co-workers, loved ones may be cut off abruptly just because their style is similar to the one who wounded us. Bitterness keeps landing on people who don't deserve it.

Through distorted decisions, damaged self-worth, and displaced dislike, the pain of that wound reaches from the past and pursues us right into the present. Indeed, bitter roots bring bitter fruit.

The replays work destructively from inside our personality, eroding our ability to love, to enjoy, even to respect ourselves. Those buried feelings are like a homeless vagrant, always looking for another place to hang out. They will have to be confronted to be conquered.

The Bible invites us to pull up those poisonous roots when it says, "Get rid of all bitterness, rage and anger, brawling and slander, along with every form of malice. Be kind and compassionate to one another, forgiving each other, just as in Christ God forgave you" (Eph. 4:31-32).

The peace word here is *forgiving*. Forgiving deflates submerged beach balls, unplugs the ugly replays.

It begins at the cross where Jesus died, as our own unworthiness sweeps over us, followed by His unconditional embrace. He has been hurt, wounded by our sin, our neglect, our rebellion. But He offers us a new beginning. We learn to forgive by being forgiven.

Using Olympic imagery, Paul proclaimed a bold, victorious approach both to the past and to the future.

Forgetting what is behind and straining toward what is ahead, I press toward the goal...(Phil. 3:13-14).

We cannot change the past. But we can change its hold on us. Freedom begins when we say, "I have read these sordid chapters of my past over and over again. I know everything that's there. I'm tired of the trash and through Jesus Christ I am turning the page to a new chapter, once and for all!"

Forgiving is the great eraser that removes the ugly pictures from the blackboards in our hearts. But those boards refuse to stay blank. Something will replace those old feelings, almost from the moment we decide to let them go.

That's why forgiving is not enough. The old root of bitterness will quickly return to fill the vacuum unless we take further action. Ephesians 4:32 couples forgiving with being "kind and compassionate to one another." Emotional liberation begins with forgiveness, but flowers when we start to *love* the person who has wronged us. Unless loving replaces the bitterness, the bitterness will return.

Jesus proposed a response for those of us who hurt that can radicalize human relationships. He told us: "Love your enemies, do good to those who hate you, bless those who curse you, pray for those who mistreat you" (Luke 6:27–28).

When we think about the person who cursed us, mistreated us, hated us, the resentment starts to rise again. And it always will, until we dare to do what Jesus said. He did more than say it—He demonstrated it on a cross. In those bitter moments, Jesus said of those who were crucifying Him, "Father, forgive them, for they do not know what they are doing" (Luke 23:34).

If "love your enemies" had come from anyone else, we might well disregard it as an emotional impossibility. But it *can* be done, it *has* been done, and it *must* be done if that tortured corner of our soul is ever going to have peace.

In Christ, we can love when we don't feel like it.

Seven Steps Toward Healing

If we are going to stop replaying the old hurts, then we will have to start rebuilding our relationship with the one who hurt us. Loving an enemy involves seven specific healing actions.

1. *Try to see the one who wounded us a wounded person.*

If you saw that person bleeding to death in front of your house, you would instinctively run to help. If you look with your heart, you might see the emotional bleeding he has been doing for a long time. He got hurt, so he hurt you. Years of unresolved anger and pain have built up inside that person and spilled all over you.

Unless you break the chain with your love and forgiveness, you will be the same way.

We have the power either to wound further by giving what "he deserved"...or to treat his wounds by giving what he needs. By reaching out to one who hurts us, we help to stop the bleeding.

If we can look past the behavior and see the wounds, we will have found a place to plant forgiveness and love.

2. *Decide to love the one who hurt you.*

Christian love is revolutionary in that it is a *choice*, not a feeling. Christ already loves the person we try to love. We decide to love him, too, and then let the Lord love him through us.

3. *Take loving action, and let the feelings follow.*

It is not hypocritical to reach out to an enemy before feeling love—it is *obedience* to the Lord's command.

Look for a compliment to give, a service to render, a special occasion to celebrate. In the process of doing things *for* those who have done things *to* us, we train our feelings toward love.

4. *Avoid doing things that antagonize the person.*

Old bitterness is rekindled by new conflicts. New conflicts are sparked by triggers that we know irritate the person we are learning to love. An emotional healer goes out of his way to head off sources of conflict. Solomon put it this way: "As charcoal to embers and as wood to fire,/so is a quarrelsome man for kindling strife" (Prov. 26:21).

When we identify and eliminate the ways we antagonize others, we become the "peacemakers" whom Jesus said were "blessed."

5. *Make the good times count.*

"*Good* times?" we react skeptically. "With *that* person? I can't think of any." If the relationship is really broken, the good moments may, in fact, be few and far between. But when we're learning to love someone, we look for times, rare as they may be, when we can talk, laugh, or play together. We even try to *create* some good times by suggesting pleasant activities we could share.

When someone has hurt us, we sometimes refuse to let there be any good times. We have given up on the person and the relationship. But love can't afford to do that. Love works to accumulate some positive new memories to replace the ugly old ones.

6. *Try to concentrate on what they do right.*

We are quick to highlight an enemy's weaknesses. We know them well. Love goes looking for *good* points as fuel for a new attitude. It's a way of seeing that gives love something to work with.

7. *Pray regularly for the person's emotional healing.*

Our hardened hearts soften as we pray for the one who wounded us. We begin to see him as God sees him, hurting because he is hurt. As a result, we begin to treat him as God treats him. Love is born on your knees.

Love is, of course, a risk. When it comes to loving an enemy, his response is unpredictable. But, then, his response doesn't really matter all that much. Our mission is to build the bridge; whether or not he crosses the bridge right now, you have done what Jesus said. That gives the Lord a lot to work with in the life of the one who wounded you.

Either way, we are free at last. That ugly root of restlessness has lost its grip on our hearts. Replaying old hurts has been replaced by rebuilding a relationship with the hurter. Forgiveness is erasing the old tapes. Love is recording new ones to take their place. Which is why the old hymnwriter wrote,

He breaks the power of cancelled sin
He sets the prisoner free...

You won't miss the shackles of bitterness. And there will
be growing instead a peaceful and quiet spot deep in your
heart, where once there was the turbulence of hate.

11

Resisting the Lord

I n a large metropolitan area it seems as if someone is always on strike. In New York we have learned to live without truck drivers, bridge tenders, even checkout personnel at the grocery store. But worst of all is when the garbage haulers go on strike.

While they negotiate, we asphyxiate. If we leave the mounting garbage bags outside, the neighborhood "critters" rip and plunder. If we leave the trash in the garage containers, it makes a lot of scents. We can spray, but the relief is just temporary. There is only one workable solution—the removal of the garbage.

As I battle the ravages of stress, I find a lot of garbage piled up in the garage of my heart. At first, I didn't even notice the smell, let alone the trash. I had accepted runaway living as "just the way it is" in a busy world.

My own showdown with stress did not begin until the smell got pretty bad. Too many days were ending with frustration, fatigue, and frayed nerves. No one could really tell. I just did not enjoy my work, my family, my friends, *myself*, as much as I used to. It wasn't the fault of those around me. If anything, they were victims of my overheated lifestyle.

It is tempting just to contain the aroma or to spray the infected air. Vacation gave me and my family a breath of the fresh air of peace. But the stink of stress still dominated everyday life. Saying no to a few commitments helped. Steps toward better organization or family priorities raised everyone's hopes for a while. But the progress proved to be a mirage.

If I was serious about peace, I concluded, I couldn't just spray. I had to *get rid of the garbage*! There is inside of us emotional trash that makes stress a chronic condition. We can't handle what is coming *at* us because of what is coming *from* us.

The change really begins when we stop blaming our *env*ironment for our frustration, and begin examining our "*in*vironment!" Thus, Jesus' words, "What comes *out of* a man is what makes him 'unclean.' For from within, out of men's hearts, come evil thoughts, sexual immorality, theft, murder, adultery, greed, malice, deceit, lewdness, envy, slander, arrogance and folly. All these evils come from *inside*" (Mark 7:20–23).

Inside is where we find the *roots* of restlessness—like reaching for more... revolving around ourselves... and replaying old hurts. It requires cleansing honesty to look in the mirror for the deepest causes of stressed-out living.

If we are unwilling to look that far for an answer, then peace will remain out of reach. Peace is *not* passive... it is an urgent pursuit—one that pursues our incurable restlessness to its roots deep inside.

The High Cost of Running

If Valium had been available in 800 B.C., Jonah could have used some! That ancient Jewish prophet was a passenger on the fast boat to Spain when a violent storm hit his ship. He was then thrown overboard by sailors hoping to appease the angry gods. At the point of drowning, he was "rescued" by a great fish that swallowed him. Contemplating being high-class fish food, Jonah must have wondered if drowning was such a bad idea after all!

On the surface, it appeared Jonah's problem all had to do with a storm and a fish. Actually, the roots went much deeper. God had given him an assignment he did not like in the enemy capital of Nineveh. His stress was a result of his resistance to the direction of God: "But Jonah ran away from the LORD" (Jon. 1:3).

When Jonah fled, God came after him. He always does. He loves us too much just to let us go. It is useless to pursue peace when God is pursuing us!

Jonah paid a high price for running from the Lord. The first chapter of Jonah reveals it cost him his money, his sleep, his prayer life, his testimony, his interest in living, and ultimately the welfare of those around him. (The people close to us always pay a price when we rebel! They get caught in our storms.)

The good news is, Jonah came back from his crisis restored, renewed, and reassigned. He got a fresh start because he recognized where the pressure was rooted...

From inside the fish Jonah prayed to the LORD his God...
"*You* hurled me into the deep [notice—not the sailors],...
all *Your* waves and breakers swept over me...
But You brought my life up from the pit" (Jon. 2:1, 3, 6).

Some of life's storms are a direct result of our disobedience. And God's attention-getting "waves and...breakers." Like Jonah, when we run *from* the Lord, we keep running *into* the Lord.

Resisting the Lord is a deep root of restlessness. If we hunger for personal peace, we must eventually stop and ask the hard question: How much of my pain is the result of resisting God?

The Battleground of Your Background

Financial debt, family conflict, physical maladies, job frustrations, disappointing relationships—a wide variety of dislocations can begin with spiritual rebellion. When we fight with the Lord, it is usually on one of three battlegrounds: Our background, "our pet" sin, or our personal plans.

Vicki fought on the battleground of her background. Raised as the daughter of a prominent minister, she was always expected to be without blemish. The spotlight on their "model" Christian family was supposed to white out any dark spots. Unfortunately, her inner struggles were only postponed until later.

Vicki quietly hated what seemed to be the narrow confinement of her family's strict standards. She knew what they were *against* more than what they were *for*. She was taught that Christians do not have feelings such as bitterness, doubt, sinful desire. Vicki had those feelings, but she denied them. There was anger toward a father she saw as depriving her, and disillusionment because his selfish private side seemed nothing like his saintly public image. But for years she lived inside the mold, seething to break out. She avoided the wrong amusements, attended the right college, and married the right boy.

Then, with a husband and a family, her ticking time bomb went off. Her material demands nearly sank the family financially; her health deteriorated in a jumble of stress related symptoms; her flagrant plunge into "worldliness" humiliated her husband; her perhaps understandable rebellion broke his heart and nearly broke their marriage.

Looking only once at Vicki might show only financial, medical, or marital stress. Looking again, more deeply, one may see Vicki, driven by restlessness rooted in resisting the Lord. She never had her adolescence as an adolescent so she had it when she was a wife and mother. Her background appeared to be the object of her rebellion. In reality, it was the Lord she was battling.

We can grow up feeling "deprived" as Vicki did if our families have a lot of don'ts. While the lights of Sodom may be off limits, they seem strangely appealing. Or, someone with a glowing religious reputation may have hurt us.

Again as we gain independence, we learn to be liberated from all those old hangups, to prove how "free" we are. But that freedom only introduces new kinds of bondage. As long as we have to prove something, we are never really free. The background we are trying to shake is actually controlling our life.

Living in reaction against our Christian background inevitably breaks Christ's heart. The Baby born in Bethlehem gets thrown out with the bath water. The scars of sin that background protected us from—even if it *over*protected—make their ugly marks now.

Saul of Tarsus had thought his personal war was against Christians. Jesus shattered that misconception when He introduced Himself on the Damascus Road: "I am Jesus, whom you are persecuting" (Acts 9:5).

While battling Christian hangups, it is all too easy to end up at war with Christ Himself. We can become, without ever meaning to, one of those Isaiah described:

"Woe to the obstinate children," declares the LORD, "to those who carry out plans that are not mine: forming an alliance, but not by My Spirit, heaping sin upon sin....These are rebellious people, deceitful children, children unwilling to listen to the LORD's instruction" (Isa. 30:1, 9).

Because of His infinite Father-love, God will pursue His fugitive children down all their dead-end streets. The stresses that came from fighting God will buffet "Jonah's" ship like no other storms on earth. The storms are not intended to blow you away, but to blow you home.

Parting with a Pet

I loved my old blue shirt. My wife did not. Yes, the shirt was faded, ripped, and permanently soiled. But those were friendly battle scars from all the duty we had seen together. Women just don't seem to understand what a man's old work clothes mean to him—that he may keep those rags until "death do us part." My wife did not wait that long.

One day I went to my closet for "old faithful," and it was gone. Panic-stricken, I called out, "Karen, where's my work shirt?"

The heartrending reply came, "I threw it out."

Our marriage is very strong. It was strong enough to survive even this disaster. But my yard work has never been the same!

It's hard to part with a pet *anything*, especially a pet sin. We all have one, and it has been with us so long that we may not even recognize it as a sin. We see past the rips and stains and consider it just part of our personalities. In reality, those pet sins form a stubborn battleground for resisting the Lord.

My "pet sin" (actually, one of several) is self-reliance, and it has been responsible for a lot of my stress. I have suffered from having the wrong people in jobs, "pushing it" financially, and running over things and people in my way—all because I was so sure I knew what *had* to be done. Pet sins always slap us with a big bill for services rendered.

As tangled as self-reliance made my life, I was blind to its sinfulness. I was hurtling forward at such a high rate of speed, the Lord had to throw big roadblocks in front of me to slow me down. And those knockdowns just compounded the pressure on my life. Finally, I have been pushed far enough beyond myself that I am ready to let the Lord clean out my closet.

We may not even see our pet sin as sin. It may well be a quiet rebellion, one that seldom surfaces in overtly evil actions. In cleaning up our spiritual houses, we may have taken out the obvious bags of garbage a long time ago. Your besetting sin may be a far more insidious concern—it may be structural damage to the whole house. Many of us are like the Prodigal Son's elder brother. We leave the Father without ever leaving the farm.

That structural damage comes in many forms—a tendency to distort or exaggerate the truth, to worry our way through life, to see the opposite sex immorally, to whine and complain (in socially acceptable ways, of course), to belittle people into doing it our way.

Whatever our pet sin, the Lord is trying to deliver us from

it. It's hard to part with a pet. But in this case, it's even harder not to.

Get With the Program

"Baby or bust"—that was Sarai's motto. Abram's wife was, according to the Book of Genesis, *determined* to be a mother, no matter what. God had promised the old couple a "miracle baby." It was taking too long by Sarai's reckoning, so she forced her own plans.

According to the customs of that time, she could be called "Mom" by a baby conceived by her husband but carried by her maidservant. Sarai gave Abram the following instructions: "Go, sleep with my maidservant; perhaps I can build a family through her" (Gen. 16:2).

The maid brought forth a son named Ishmael, and Sarai's plan worked, for a while. *God's* plan was fulfilled when Sarai herself got pregnant and bore Isaac. The children of Isaac are today's Jews, the children of Ishmael are today's Arabs. The conflict between them is still tearing the world apart four thousand years later!

The Sarai Syndrome is still with us today. When we insist on *our* plans, we often find ourselves on another battleground for resisting the Lord. And the results are usually disastrous.

Most of us have a deeply personal blueprint that begins with the words, "I'll find a way." It may read, "I'll find a way..."
- To get married
- To own the house or the car I want
- To get the position I want
- To make my children what I want them to be
- To leave my church and make the pastor look bad
- To leave my ministry and make the board look bad
- To get out of this house.

The resistance to God comes at the point of His delaying or denying our plan. So we determine that no one will get in our way, including God.

Becky was a woman with one nonnegotiable "I'll find a way." She was going to be married, no matter what. She thought God was taking too long. She got married—twice, in fact. In both cases, the most available prospects were not Christians. Becky swallowed her personal faith to make her plans happen. The first marriage lasted one agonizing year. Her second marriage has been riddled with conflict over church attendance, spiritual training for the children, ways to earn money, and countless values choices.

When we push for our plans, we may get what we plan for ...and reap a bitter harvest. Peace comes from fitting into God's plans. Stress comes from trying to fit God into our plans.

"Get with the program" is good advice if it is *His* program. As a lifelong planner and a male counterpart to Sarai, I am enjoying letting Him drive. My driving has driven me right into the ground. It's nice to relax and enjoy the ride for a change.

God's Good Goads

"He goaded me into it." Those words explain a lot of unplanned changes in our lives. He had not planned to fix that leaky faucet yet but his wife goaded him into it. She had not planned to have her daughter's friend sleep over tonight— she goaded her mother into it. Since we are so often goaded, we should know what a goad is.

It goes back to the ancient farmer whose John Deere was an ox, strong but stubborn. When the old ox reached the end of one crop row, he had no intention of turning around to plow another one. That is why the farmer carried a long stick with a spade at one end and a point on the other—a goad. If his ox refused to turn, he got the point! If the animal moved at the farmer's gentle nudge, there was no need for the goad. Pain came from resistance.

The apostle Paul knew about goads. He learned about them on the day the Lord confronted him on the Damascus Road. Jesus simply pointed out to that rebellious rabbi, "It is hard for you to kick against the goads" (Acts 26:14).

Centuries earlier, Solomon had observed: "The words of the wise are like goads, their collected sayings like firmly embedded nails—given by one Shepherd" (Eccles. 12:11).

If we feel the pain of God's good goads, running will not help. God uses the goad when we will not turn His direction.

The roots of our restlessness may go deep into resisting the Lord. Reacting against our background, coddling our "pet sins," insisting on our plans all make life more turbulent. Thus, Isaiah wrote:

"I am the LORD your God,
who teaches you what is best for you,
who directs you in the way you should go.
If only you had paid attention to My commands,
your peace would have been like a river" (Isa. 48:17–18).

12

Rushing the Process

I'm not much for bumper stickers, but I loved one my wife pointed out to me on the Interstate a while back. It simply declared: "One Day at a Time."

It became even more meaningful when my lead foot pulled us alongside that car in the passing lane. One quick glance told the story behind the sticker. A mother was driving with her young son, and he was moving erratically inside the car. His head was oversized, his features distorted—he was severely retarded. Glancing in the rearview mirror at my three healthy children in the back seat, I got a lump in my throat over that woman's special burden. "One Day at a Time" was much more than a bumper sticker for her—it was a way of life!

No matter what the weight of our burdens, that is how we were built to live. That is why Jesus taught us both about daily bread (see Matt. 6:11) and taking up our cross daily (see Luke 9:23). Any peaceful strategy for living must be committed to handling life in twenty-four hour, bite-size chunks. We strain ourselves when we try to carry more than the weight of today.

Any peace-pursuer must be struck by the promise of the Psalms, "The meek will inherit the land/And *enjoy great peace*" (Ps. 37:11). In the ten verses preceding that promise, the "meek" are told three times, "Do not fret" (vv. 1, 7, 8).

Worry is the archenemy of personal peace, and worry begins when we reach ahead into tomorrow's troubles and bring them into today.

We insist on living with the concerns of next month's bread and next year's cross. We squander our peace on the "mights" and "what ifs" of our future. Instead of taking life one day at a time, we are prone to *rushing the process*, another unsettling root of restlessness.

Paralyzed

Disturbing the peace is a crime, and it should be. Worry is an emotional crime because, like a noisy neighbor, it keeps disturbing the peace. The dictionary bluntly says that worry is "to torment oneself with disturbing thoughts"—self-torment!

Jesus warned us against rushing tomorrow when He said: "Do not worry about tomorrow, for tomorrow will worry about itself. *Each day has enough trouble of its own*" (Matt. 6:34). In other words, deal with stress in twenty-four hour compartments! We're over our heads when we go for more than that.

In fact, Jesus carried his worry-warnings even further when He told us, "The worries of this life...choke the word, making it unfruitful" (Mark 4:19).

Rushing the process creates a major log jam in God's ability to get through! His Master Plan is an unfolding scroll, to be revealed a day at a time. When we try to unroll it faster, we succumb to stress.

Worry creates *paralysis*. I feel paralyzed when I am confronted with a desk full of mail, a file full of overdue correspondence, a calendar full of onrushing deadlines, and a room full of people needing to see me. One of my greatest mathematical curiosities is how I can go away for *one* week and be *three* weeks behind. It never fails!

A student knows the paralyzed feeling of term papers, reading assignments, exams, and work hours all crashing in at once. And no one juggles more crisis management than a homemaker. Laundry, little ones, luncheons, and loose ends challenge her to decide, "Where will I *start?*"

Because we often do not know where to start, we don't. We look at the pile and become frustrated. By running ahead mentally to *everything* that needs to be done, we lose the poise to do *something*. And the deadlines keep coming. The Bible speaks about the paralysis of worry when it observes that "Whoever watches the wind will not plant;/whoever looks at the clouds will not reap" (Eccles. 11:4). We can only work full speed if we concentrate on today's planting, not all the possibilities of the days ahead.

Too Quick to Panic

Worry also creates *panic*. Burdened by all the disastrous "what-ifs," we tend to react rather than act.

There are enough "teen-age problem" books and headlines, for example, to stampede the most confident parent. Fearing the worst, it is easy to overreact to an adolescent's natural muscle flexing.

Lynn's parents panicked when their daughter showed her first interest in Rick. Because he was not a Christian like Lynn, they feared everything from her losing her virginity to her losing her faith. Actually, Lynn was only "trying on" this relationship—she was not serious about Rick. But Mom and Dad reacted as if they were serious, virtually declaring war on their romance.

Lynn was humiliated by her parents' treatment of Rick and offended by their lack of trust in her. She leaped to Rick's defense, determined to show her parents she could make her own decisions. The harder Mom and Dad fought, the closer Lynn and Rick got. By reacting to all that *could* happen, Lynn's parents *made* it happen.

A wise parent takes his child's friends, music, moods, and flirtations one day at a time. In the relaxed atmosphere of today, parents can ask good questions instead of firing prosecutor's accusations: respect their friends rather than inspecting them; give them space rather than smothering their growth. Knowing where bad choices can go should cause a parent to handle with care, not with heavy artillery.

Panic can literally cause us to worry ourselves sick. Obsession with disease can help give disease a foothold. While the connection between stress and illness is still under study, it is clear that stress can contribute to such damaging conditions as high blood pressure, lung ailments, heart trouble, and even cancer. The stress of worrying about health may do more harm than any disease will ever do. That is why the Bible makes this connection between stress and health: "Banish anxiety from your heart and cast off the troubles of your body" (Eccles. 11:10).

Parenting and personal health are only two of life's many temptations to hit the panic button. Being single "too long," getting justice for unfair treatment, being left behind at work, running out of money someday—countless fears tempt us to rush ahead. In each case, however, grabbing for tomorrow's troubles today will expose us to the perils of panic. Fearing an outcome may actually help it to happen.

Most "mights" never happen. If they do happen the Lord will give us the grace to handle them the day they come. In other words, *worry is a waste of time*!

Handoffs and Mountain Trails

Quarterbacks make good money. They should, with the monsters they have to get away from every time the football is snapped. As soon as the signal-caller gets the ball, at least a half-ton of opposing linemen come after him. Every quarterback knows how to get rid of the pressure—get rid of the *ball*. He learns the happy art of the handoff, giving the pigskin to a passing halfback or fullback. When you hand off the ball, you put the pressure on someone else!

That's why daily praying is a key to confident one-day living. As your day begins, you hand off the anticipated pressures to God's hands. As your day unfolds, you hand off the ones you didn't anticipate, too. You let go of that ball of stress, and let *Him* take the pressure. God invited us to...

not be anxious about anything, but in everything, by prayer and peti-
tion, with thanksgiving, present your requests to God [the handoff!].
And the *peace* of God, which transcends all understanding, will guard
your hearts and your minds in Christ Jesus (Phil 4:6-7).

Our family was vacationing in the Adirondacks, and we
mobilized ourselves one summer afternoon for the hike up
Chimney Mountain. By the halfway point, we had put in a
good day's exercise. Karen, who had been pointing out to us
all the scenic beauty along the way, made a suggestion.
"This has been a beautiful hike, hasn't it? Let's start back."

I couldn't believe my ears. Start back? The purpose of
climbing a mountain is to get to the *top*. I argued that all this
energy was wasted unless we reached the summit. My wife
responded, "I thought the purpose of climbing a mountain is
to enjoy the scenery."

The fact is, both points of view were valid. But many of us
are panting and pushing for the *destination*, while God is also
concerned with the *process*. We fast-food/instant-tea rushers
often run ahead of the careful, perfectly synchronized plans
of God.

Like baking bread, you rush it, you ruin it.

Daily progress is a peaceful way to measure our lives, con-
verting *long-term goals into short-term achievements*. If you want
to spend more time with the family, spend exclusive time (no
matter how brief) with each one *today*. If you plan to "get out
of debt," clip some coupons and stay within your food
budget at the store *today*. If you intend to "buckle down this
semester," take good notes and review the lecture *today*. Your
promise to "get closer to God this year" can best be served
by recording in a diary *this morning's* time with the Lord.

Your confidence grows as you concentrate on what got
done today. And you don't waste energy on what you did not
get done...that progress is for another day.

One day at a time is a liberating way to live. I think back
over all the days I have concluded with a gnawing dissatisfaction, a corrosive anxiety. My mind was constantly racing,
obsessed with all that was not finished and with all the fore-

boding possibilities of tomorrow.

On the pathway to peace, I am learning something better. I do what I can in a day—and leave it at that. I hand off the "mights" to my Father and give my very best to the realities of this day. Period. My days are as full as ever, but I take them one at a time. I'm getting a lot more done.

Real Healing

Stress control is a lot like weight control. Temporary improvement is easy, but permanent change requires a new way of living. You can patch things up, slow things down, treat folks better for a little while—only to get out of control again in a few months.

I want something more lasting than that. And so do all of us.

God has been leading me through a process to real healing. Fatigued and frustrated, I first had been able to identify stress as the issue. Little did I realize how far I would have to go to find the roots of my restlessness.

In digging at the roots of stress, I have learned a hope-filled secret: if you deal with the stress that comes *from* you, you can handle any stress that comes *at* you. In Christ, we are more than able to replace:

- Reaching for more, with contentment
- Revolving around ourselves, with "giving living"
- Replaying old hurts, with loving forgiveness
- Resisting the Lord, with obedience
- Rushing the process, with "one day" living.

With those weeds uprooted, we can begin to grow flowers. It is, in fact, those weeds that have always choked the most glorious bloom in our garden...personal peace.

Once we sample that peace, we will never again miss those old roots. We are finally living in peace...where we were meant to live.

Part IV
Attacking the Stress Centers

13

Taking the Offensive

As you drive north toward the wilderness of Canada, first the expressways run out, then the pavement, and finally the back roads. At that desolate point, there is a thought-provoking sign:

Choose your rut carefully—you'll be in it for the next 50 miles.

I have considered posting signs like that all over my house, my car, my phone, my datebook, and my office. There are far more ruts in our daily civilization than there are in the Canadian wilderness! And we have not chosen our ruts very carefully, if we chose them at all. I have been in some "life ruts" for far more than fifty miles and never even realized I was in them.

"A fixed and dull or unpromising way of life"—that is how the dictionary defines a rut. When I decided to pursue personal peace aggressively, I began to see a lot of "unpromising ways of life" we had accumulated.

Peace had not dropped in on me in one gift-wrapped bundle. It was, and is, unfolding as I take strong corrective and preventive action. It began as a cry for change that came from my tired body and my restless heart.

Every time I heard the word "peace," something jumped inside me. As I pursued it through the Bible, I discovered—

or rediscovered—how to "fill 'er up" with inner calm each day. Peace develops as we...Protect the Quiet Centers.

Much to my surprise, my search led beyond the roots of peace—to the roots of restlessness. Underneath the surface *symptoms* of stress, there were inner *diseases* which had to be faced. The tentacles of stress began to loosen as I learned that peace pursuers must...Remove the Roots of Restlessness.

Having confronted the stress that was coming from me, I was ready to do something about the stress that was coming at me. My wife and I convened the first of many "summit conferences" to identify the "ruts" in our life. We asked each other, "What sources of pressure keep taking over ...and how can we control them?"

All of us face life crises that we cannot control: financial setbacks, the death or divorce of someone close, a long, lonely season, the fickleness of friends, the upheaval from an accident or an illness. If our life is already out of control, there is no room for the unexpected. People living with a glass already full will overflow when these heavy doses come. Even the small surprises—flat tires, broken appliances, unexpected drop-ins, a late delivery—will cause a messy spill.

If we control our *everyday* sources of stress, we will have room for the *extraordinary* stresses. That realization launched a "search-and-destroy" mission in my life, to find and conquer those persistent sources of pressure, conflict, and frustration. I knew them well. They growled at me regularly. If I want personal peace, I have to—

Attack the Stress Centers

That attack is focused on eight everyday trouble spots.

1. *Organize the confusing corners.*

My library was depressing. It has long ago outgrown our small bookcases and its once-neat categories. Finding a book, whether for myself or friends in need, had become a horrible new way to waste time. That confusing corner of my life was one of those countless "pinpricks" that kept tormenting me. For me, the answer was simple. We finally built bigger bookcases and organized those hopeless stacks into easy-to-find sections. Exit, a little stress!

Our lives are full of those confusing corners. They erode our ability to handle "the big stuff." Those "disorderlies" in our lives cause stress when we just *look* at them! Order and peace are linked together when Scripture says: "God is not a God of disorder but of peace" (1 Cor. 14:33).

A confusing corner may be that closet that keeps overflowing into the room. Or drawers stuffed with outgrown clothes that could give us space and give a friend's child the clothes he needs. Or the chaotic garage that could provide both storage space and work space if it were organized.

We really believe in the value of vitamins at our house. Unfortunately, they were getting far too much attention. The hassle of finding and reminding got on everybody's nerves. I was amazed at the difference five muffin tins could make. My wife set up one for each of us with our names and each day marked on it, and fourteen days' worth of vitamins. It works! No more morning bottle sorting.

Our attack on little stress centers led Karen to organize the "creative clutter" of her slide stacks. Now she can locate them quickly when certain slides are needed for media shows or book covers. She has also attacked the trail of baseball cards strung through the house by starting "Mom's collection" from any cards left out and lying around. We also found stress jumping out of the refrigerator at us as long-forgotten foods evolved into dangerous new life forms. Stick-on labels now help us keep track of surprises in both the refrigerator and the freezer.

Not all the confusing corners are at home. A student, for example, feels the bombardment of the calendars and demands of six different teachers. The syllabi and exams and projects and papers can blur into a swirl of stress *or* be organized on a chart of deadlines and weekly progress.

Offices have confusing corners that keep attacking, too. A secretary friend got tired of the daily search through the "accounts payable" folder. She simplified her life simply by filing invoices in separate alphabetical folders.

There have been days when the stack on my desk threatened to devour me. That corner is far less confusing now that my three baskets—in, out, and priority—are working. The priority basket prevents worry about the urgency of my in box, and the pressure of missing something pressing.

Most confusing corners can be organized through simple adjustments. They need to be faced—then fixed. We have walked by them too many times and let them dog us. It's time we called the dog-catcher—or Solomon might have called them "the little foxes."

Catch for us the foxes, the little foxes that ruin the vineyards (Song of Sol. 2:15).

2. *Control the time wasters.*

"Give me a twenty-eight hour day, or better yet an eight-day week!" For years that was my battle cry. I thought more time was the answer. Since that is an unlikely prospect, a more likely solution is making better use of the time we have! The time we *want* is probably available in the time we *waste.* Solomon's clear-minded wisdom shows through again when he observed: "There is a time for everything, and *a season for every activity* under heaven:...He [God] has made everything beautiful *in its time*" (Eccles. 3:1, 11).

That sounds simple enough, but most overcrowded lives violate those guidelines. Time wasters are usually good, or at least neutral, aspects of our lives. They have quietly exceeded their "season" or their "beautiful time" and destroyed the balance we once had. It's our natural *tendency toward addiction* that gobbles up time we could use more constructively. We succumb to "too much of a good thing."

For example, we decide to fight physical fatness with physical fitness. Even our coping with stress is enhanced as we walk, jog, exercise, bicycle, play sports. Then, without even noticing, we let "enough" grow to "more than enough." We sacrifice valuable family time, God time, or work time for too much of a good thing.

You can get lost in a hobby or a workshop, leaving, for all practical purposes, a widowed partner and orphaned children. Plants and pets can take up too much time; so can antiques, flea markets, and sports events.

We cancelled about half the magazines that flooded our mailbox monthly—not because they were bad, but because there were too many. Our attack on time wasters even reached my wife's plants. I had often suggested to Karen that they could film the next Tarzan movie at our house. Our living room jungle began with cuttings offered to us by friends. Unfortunately, they all grew. As we streamlined our lives, Karen gave away a lot of those plants because of the time they were taking. We are left with fewer, bigger plants. And Tarzan will have to go somewhere else to find Cheetah!

The title for "Heavyweight Time Waster of the World" probably goes to that chubby fellow in the corner, the television set. We have all experienced conversation in a roomful of people when the "tube" was talking, too. One by one, eyes and attention drifted from the conversation to the TV. Soon, the whole room was hypnotized.

It is that hypnotic quality that enables TV to be such an insidious time waster. You turn it on to watch one show, and drift lazily into the next one and the next one. You channel-hop for a minute and get hooked for an hour.

If you want to dethrone King Television, your local viewing guide can be a big help. Our family has learned to look at it together at the beginning of the week and decide in advance what is worth watching. We waste far less time if we select our shows with the TV off.

Controlling our flickering blue friend was so important to us that we decided to reward our kids for it. Every week they receive five "TV pennies," each redeemable at the end of the week for fifty cents. Whenever a child watches thirty minutes of television, he forfeits a TV penny—and fifty cents. That extra $2.50 a week has reactivated a lot of books, games, and exercises, not to mention homework!

King David modeled for us a prayer for balance in our crowded lives:

Teach us to number our days aright, that we may gain a heart of wisdom (Ps. 90:12).

3. *Restrict the terrible twins.*

Some people wait eagerly for their telephone or doorbell to ring. At our place, we wait for them to stop ringing. For us, and for many similarly saturated people, the phone and the doorbell are the terrible twins. No matter what we're doing, they barge in without checking. If they are not controlled, they will control you.

Before I began my plan for peace, I took most calls when they came. In so doing, I often compromised time I had committed and lost concentration on a project. Now I am learning to designate a time when I will return all my calls for the day, except for emergencies. As a result, both my work and my caller get better attention.

At home, the dinner hour has taken on new importance as we try to protect a quiet center. In most cases, we greet the dinner hour caller warmly and encourage him to call back in half an hour. Our family faith time is generally phone-proofed too.

When someone comes to the door at a priority time, we do not, of course, ask him to call back later. My wife has mastered the art of welcoming a visitor and including that person in whatever she is doing. Many visits can coexist with ironing or dishwashing; they don't always have to preempt the previously scheduled program. We try to encourage folks to give us a call before they come over. Over the years we have had a parade of teen-agers drop in on us at the craziest times. I have tried to retrain them by taking a few minutes with them but suggesting, "I wish you had called. I could have set aside more time for us to talk."

While learning to restrict the terrible twins, everyone at home and at the office needs to practice two important cautions. First, be alert for the person who needs to talk *now*.

Many, if not most, callers or visitors could talk a little later, if necessary. But some cannot wait. We never lose ground for dropping everything to grab a needy hand.

Secondly, every caller or visitor should feel special, no matter when they ring. A follower of Christ lives a lifestyle where, "Love covers over a multitude of sins [even intrusions]. Offer hospitality to one another without grumbling" (1 Pet. 4:8-9).

Controlling interruptions does not mean cutting off people! It can, however, make the difference between their getting the best or grudging leftovers. Taming the telephone and the doorbell casts a vote for sanity. Without boundaries, the terrible twins are tyrants.

4. *Lower the raised voices*.

It was New Year's Eve, and we were having a down-home family celebration. Instead of party hats and noisemakers, I handed out construction paper and markers to everyone. On each person's sheet I had spelled "Happy New Year" down the side in acrostic form. Then we each composed resolutions to begin with those twelve letters. We had unforgettable times sharing them then, and reviewing them the following New Year's Eve.

My first *E* came from my new pursuit of peace: "Eliminate yelling as a form of communication at our house." I knew it was a big goal, but a biblical one!

A gentle answer turns away wrath, but a harsh word stirs up anger (Prov. 15:1).
Reckless words pierce like a sword, but the tongue of the wise brings healing (Prov. 12:18).

Very few gentle or healing words are said with a raised voice. Yelling escalates anger and creates a stress center worthy to be attacked. One soft voice can lower the rising temperature almost immediately.

People usually yell as a form of verbal shorthand. When there isn't much time to get a point across, we say it loudly. Ironically, louder ends up longer. The message may be heard

but not understood and we have to slow down later and re-
state it. And while a raised voice may get the immediate desired result, it may also inflict a wound. Treating that wound
will take a lot more time than lowering the voice.

The person who determines to speak gently takes a giant
step toward de-stressing his environment. In biblical terms,
he is a conqueror: "Better a patient man than a warrior: a
man who controls his temper than one who takes a city"
(Prov. 16:32).

5. *Fix the floating boundaries.*

From a distance, they might be mistaken for two-legged
zebras. Actually, they are the men who keep many football
games from becoming World War III. Without those referees, the game would devolve into chaos. Fortunately, they
do not have to make the rules or decide the boundaries.
They only enforce what has been decided in advance.

Many a family or business could profit from their example. Confusion and stress result when the rules, the boundaries, and the penalties keep changing. If, however, those
guidelines are clear in advance, and consistent in application, everyone can concentrate on the game. That is why the
Bible connects domestic refereeing with peace: "Discipline
your son, and he will give you peace; he will bring delight to
your soul" (Prov. 29:17).

We have a well-written manual of policies and procedures
at our office. Because some of the enforcement responsibilities have been unclear, we have sometimes ended up making
our own individual policies. The result has been, of course,
inconvenience, misunderstanding, and inefficiency. When
we fixed the floating boundaries, everyone felt more secure.

Home is where boundaries tend to float most freely. Children do not know whether the whistle will blow when they
first cross the white line or when they are out of the stadium.
And they often lack the predictable structure that develops
confidence.

Making a decision every time an issue arises adds stress.
When you settle a lot of issues in advance, you eliminate

stress. Consistency is born from Mom and Dad's agreeing on family policies so that the kids don't hear two drummers. It is the responsibility of the "Leadership Team" to be sure there are three specific guidelines.

First, clear boundaries must be set. What is "out of bounds" when it comes to curfew, homework, time to obey, language, music, arguing? Children need a strong signal as to how far is too far. We have happier children at our house when we stick to our one-time policy. They know that one finger is a reminder that the second call is too late.

Second, clear penalties must be established. Tension escalates whenever parents have to decide a penalty in the middle of an overheated incident. Many problems can be anticipated and the consequences discussed quietly and objectively. Then, like the referees, parents only enforce the penalty.

Third, clear responsibilities must be assigned. "Work before play" is a peace policy at our house. Chores are spelled out, along with a deadline for having them done. The fun begins when the work is done.

We also found that our boys were as tired as we were of the morning nagging about teeth, clean clothes, and combed hair. The checklist on the back of the door eliminated many reminders and provided needed structure.

At home and at work we all have a lot more profitable things to talk about than the same old frictions. Everyone feels better when the boundaries get fixed.

6. *Eliminate the double signals.*

As the tour boat approached Fort Sumter, I reflected on an amusing question. What color uniforms would the Civil War guides be wearing? Sumter had been a Union fort in Confederate territory when the Civil War began there in 1861. It had changed hands several times, thus causing me to wonder whether we would see a blue or gray uniform. Henry Kissinger must have decided the colors. We were greeted at the gate by a "soldier" wearing a blue coat and gray pants! That uniform might be a good idea now, but it would not have worked very well back in 1861. The poor man would have gotten shot on both ends!

In a moral sense, it is not a very good idea to wear two uniforms either. When a follower of Christ sends double signals to his world, he draws fire from both sides. Many a believer "changes uniforms" when his Christian standards become too costly. The irony is that compromise increases stress over the long haul.

When people are not sure of our stand, they keep pushing. If we sometimes "lie for the company" and sometimes not, the boss will continue to press. If, however, we consistently stick to the truth, the pressure will let up after a series of initial tests. Wherever we are, our reputations eventually protect us from the constant pressure to go to the wrong places, to laugh at the wrong things, to pass on the gossip. People will accept us for who we are—once we accept ourselves.

Consistency will diminish the stress within as well as around. The guilt, the deception, the halfheartedness tears us apart. The double-minded man is, in the words of the Bible, "unstable in all he does" (James 1:8). When you wear one uniform proudly, you only draw fire from one side. The other side will respect you enough to hold its fire most of the time.

7. *Swallow the verbal irritants.*

My quest for personal peace was launched on the words of David: "Seek peace and pursue it" (Ps. 34:14).

There is a warning that precedes that challenge—one that is a key to realizing it. David, a man who had suffered so much abuse from King Saul, tied peace to this caution: "Keep your tongue from evil" (Ps. 34:13).

When Peter quoted David's invitation to pursue peace, he prefaced it this way: "Do not repay evil with evil or insult with insult, but with blessing" (1 Pet. 3:9). The Bible is clear. To add peace, we must subtract the words that hurt people. For me, that meant some vocabulary inventory. Perhaps because I was carrying such a full glass, I would too often resort to sentences guaranteed to irritate.

I would watch my children aggravate each other with jokes, horseplay, and teasing carried too far. They pushed until someone exploded. I hated what I was seeing, especially when I realized they had learned it from me. Aggravation was a verbal irritant, a stress center I could control.

Some of our irritants are weapons to get our way. One well-placed sarcastic remark can level the opposition. The poison is so venomous that it affects both the giver and the receiver. If we win with wounds like those, have we really won?

Guilt is another withering weapon. We know the words, the look that will make people bow right now—and make them bitter later on.

We are trying at our house to notice how one person's negative comment can make the whole place dark. The complaint about dinner, the put-down of clothes or ability, the caustic comeback all serve to irritate. And irritated people inevitably create a stress-charged atmosphere. In an office, a dormitory, or a family, the nay-sayer can cover everyone's sunshine with a gloom cloud.

When Peter wrote about not repaying evil with evil, he was identifying the match for verbal fireworks. In sports like volleyball and tennis, the object is to return the other person's shot. In playing for peace, we refuse to return someone's shot. We do not respond in like kind. In spite of all we want to say, the verbal volley stops.

When we swallow the verbal irritants, we exercise great peace power. And we take another step toward Paul's advice:

If it is possible, as far as it depends on you, live at peace with everyone (Rom. 12:18).

8. *Limit the competing agendas.*

To cross the Hudson River from New Jersey into Manhattan one can choose between two long tunnels that go under the river or one long bridge that goes over it. The Hudson is wide when it reaches Manhattan, but not very powerful.

But the Hudson is a much different river near its head-

waters in upstate New York. There it roars along with a driving, even dangerous current. Upstate its banks are confined,
and its force is greater. By the time it reaches Manhattan,
the Hudson is so spread out that its power seems almost
gone.

People peter out the same way: they get too spread out.
They accumulate commitments instead of making choices—
they add new arenas without removing any old ones. Homework fights it out with household chores, extracurriculars,
youth meetings, and music lessons. A businessman says yes
until his resumé looks impressive but his contributions are
insignificant. An overcommitted woman needs a valet just to
manage all her hats—wife, mother, committee worker, volunteer, career person, creator, entertainer. By taking on
more than we can possibly do well, we live in direct violation
of God's command to "make it your ambition to lead a quiet
life" (1 Thess. 4:11).

My wife and children have followed all too well in my
overextended footsteps. Somewhere on the way to peace, I
decided all these competing agendas were swirling stress centers. And they could be controlled by that most powerful
two-letter word, *no*. It was a word Jesus knew how to say.

When the sun was setting, the people brought to Jesus all who had var-
ious kinds of sickness, and...He healed them....At daybreak Jesus
went out to a solitary place. The people were looking for Him
and...they tried to keep Him from leaving them. But He said, "I
must preach the good news of the kingdom of God to the other towns
also, because that is why I was sent" (Luke 4:40-43).

There were still plenty of people to heal, but Jesus said no.
He had settled the "I musts" of His life—in this case preaching to the other towns. Having settled His yeses, He could
say no to anything that would compromise them.

In attacking the stress center of competing agendas, I had
to set some priorities to plan by. I said yes to the spiritual
leadership of my family. As area director of Youth for Christ,
I committed myself to strengthening our local ministry for

the long-term future, and to an expanded preaching ministry. Although I had long anticipated a broad-based evangelism crusade in our area, I had to resign from the executive
committee that was finally planning one. It just did not fit in
with the priorities.

Those choices were further tested when I was asked to
stand for re-election to the National Board of Youth for
Christ. Since these trustees are elected by all our staff, it is a
very high honor. It also carries with it the privilege of working with some prominent lay leaders and helping to mold national policy.

As Karen and I prayed together about it, I said, "It
doesn't fit, does it, honey?" After declining the nomination,
I was contacted by several surprised national leaders. One
just doesn't turn down this position, but I had to.

I am learning a way to sort out my choices. It helps me to
ask: "Could someone else do this just as well? Is this a spot
God has uniquely qualified me for? Or is it something many
others could do?" Unless my ego has deceived me into thinking I'm God's gift to everyone, that kind of thinking can settle a lot of priorities.

Where can we do the most with our gifts? We must limit
ourselves to the few things we can really do well. It is better
to make a big mark in a few places than a little mark in a lot
of places.

We need to pass that kind of wisdom on to our children,
too. In the superkid syndrome, they choose activities as if
they were ordering in a Chinese restaurant: one from
Column A, two from Column B, and some from every other
column on the menu.

Kids should try on a variety of experiences in school,
learning lots of ways to enjoy life. But they should not try on
everything at the same time! It is a parent's responsibility to
help children learn priority thinking at any early age, to limit
those competing agendas that eventually split us like a wishbone.

"No" gives us the blessed freedom to enjoy our commitments. And the concentrated power of a stream in narrow banks.

Stress centers are as deeply entrenched as ruts in the wilderness road. Their power is not broken by pills or promises. They must be attacked. That is part of the adventure of reorganizing life around the pursuit of peace. You cultivate peace in the quiet centers while retaking the ground that stress has held for so long.

There is great wisdom in the old Greek motto that says, "You will break the bow if you keep it always bent." It feels good to remember again how to relax the bow—to let the tension go at last. A life under control is a bow that will last a lifetime.

Part V
Establishing Peaceful Habits

14

Peaceful People Habits

I don't ever want to weigh 210 pounds again.

Carrying that much weight on my 5' 8" frame, I looked like the Goodyear Blimp II. While I may not be a "hunk" at my current 150 pounds, at least I'm not a chunk! I have maintained this mini-me for enough years that most of my friends say, "I can't *imagine* your being that fat!" I really was that heavy. And I could be again.

My metabolism is still the same one that made "a moment on the lips, forever on the hips." Getting thin has not been the problem, of course. It is *staying* thin. If I did not want to go back to the fat old days, I needed more than a diet. I needed entirely new eating habits.

I cannot live the rest of my life eating grapefruit and celery. But I learned to eat a light lunch; save my fun food for more active days; stop eating after 6:00 P.M.; and plan for Christmas cookies with a pre–holiday diet.

My concerns about personal peace have a lot in common with my concerns about personal pounds. I am in much better shape emotionally, enough for those close to me to notice. By protecting those quiet centers and attacking stress at its roots, I feel much lighter. But I also know that I could put all of the weight of stress right back on. After all, my emotional metabolism has not greatly changed, either. I can still convert pressure into stress and tension as quickly as my body turns food into fat. Everybody likes the new me better, including me. I do not want to go back to being emotionally overweight ever again!

New habits are the key to lasting change. After restoring order and sanity to our lives, we need daily behavior patterns to maintain the progress. The final, decisive lap in the pursuit of personal peace is to *establish peaceful habits.*

These habits create a structure in which peace flourishes. They are the product of wise choices, the kind Solomon described when he said: "Blessed is the man who finds wisdom,...her ways are pleasant ways, and all her paths are peace" (Prov. 3:13, 17). Wisdom, in other words, always chooses the lifestyle that will lead to peace. In this chapter, I want to discuss these wise, peaceful habits as they relate to people—for dealing with others and ourselves. In the following chapter, we'll talk about peaceful habits in our work—the things we do.

Consistently practiced, these habits become "peace insurance." They are the emotional nutrition and exercise that *keep* us in good shape. Since people are more important than tasks, we begin with the habits that affect our

Peace with People.

Offer Your Availability

There are people who want to be noticed by us—people we live with, work with, worship with. We have two choices. We can offer ourselves to them, or, make them pursue us. To make yourselves available to them is far most Christlike, and more peaceful.

When it comes to seeking attention, kids are the experts. It is not that they necessarily need it more, they are just more overt in going for it. They can find an infinite number of excuses for interrupting after they have just gotten home or you have. Their list includes everything from trivial questions, to pressing needs, to permission requested. In many cases, they only want us to know they are *there!* If we let them know that as soon as we see them, we can both avoid the stress of these emotional charades.

While adults are a little more subtle, they, too, will push for time which should have been offered. Strangely enough, they usually need less of our time if we take the initiative. Our mates need to be talked to and touched right away. Our co-workers need a "How was your weekend?" or a "How's your wife feeling?" Our friends want a little recognition and interest.

The busier we are, the more we may want to avoid reaching out. In reality, by reaching out, we usually end up with more time.

Some of the pressure we all feel is from people who can't find us. So they keep trying. Doctors solve that by having call-in hours; professors by posting office hours. Stress is added to life when we are always available, never available, or unpredictably available. We will be pursued less if people *know when they can reach us*. My wife loves sentences like, "Tuesday morning is all yours."

When the people close to me can depend on seeing me, we all have more peace.

Tear Down Walls

In those classic old Westerns, the marshal could be counted on to tell Bad Bart, "I want you out of town by sundown!" "Out by sundown" is God's plan for all of us keeping our town peaceful. He said: "Do not let the sun go down while you are still angry" (Eph. 4:26).

Peace is anchored to the determination *not to let any conflict last until tomorrow*. And that determination requires hard work and constant vigilance: "*Make every effort* to keep the unity of the spirit through the bond of peace" (Eph. 4:3).

Paul stressed that same work-for-it commitment when he told us to "*Make every effort* to do what leads to peace" (Rom. 14:19). Three "efforts" will help keep the peace in any relationship.

First, deal with conflict quickly and initially. Disney

World must be the cleanest amusement park in the world. Everywhere you go, you see Disney workers cleaning up. It seems that they would catch any cup you dropped before it hit the ground. That park is clean because they *don't let a mess get started*.

When that principle governs relationships, bad feelings are headed off while they are small. It is all too easy to ignore a "little" strain, only to find it growing into something very ugly later on. Tear down a potential wall while it is still just a brick or two tall!

Second, tell how you feel. I never knew I was hurting my wife—until she finally told me. Without realizing it, I was frequently interrupting or correcting her conversation in public. When I knew, I stopped. Many times I don't *tell* how I'm feeling because I *expect* other people to know. Unfortunately, they don't. Most of us have radar with very limited range.

A judgmental accusation is the world's *least effective* means of sharing feelings: "You're too busy to listen to me!" It guarantees a defensive reaction and more disagreement. Walls are best avoided by a statement in the first person: "I just don't feel really heard or understood right now."

Third, admit being wrong. If a broken marriage or friendship or parent-child relationship could be X-rayed, an ugly dark spot might show up: someone who could not be wrong. There are no harder, yet more healing words in the English language than "I was wrong." If we can genuinely apologize, no matter what the response, we can destroy the bricks from which walls are made.

Practice Cheerleading

Until last season, our local high school football team had forgotten how to win. As the year progressed, the number of fans dwindled steadily down to the most loyal parents. Yet no matter how badly our players fared, one group always had something good to say about them—the cheerleaders. Not once did they pack up their megaphones and desert to the other side or start yelling, "Our boys are real bums!" A good word from the cheerleaders can always be counted on, win or lose.

Our world is suffering from a severe cheerleader shortage. While I have no plans to wear a letter sweater and a short skirt, I *do* want to be a cheerleader. The typical home or business or school has enough *jeer*leaders—people who tell folks about weaknesses and shortcomings they already know too much about. We need *positive* people who look for the good in a person and tell what they see: "The lips of the righteous nourish many" (Prov. 10:21).

I am convinced people feel small most of the time. A cheerleader is determined to make each family member, each friend feel big each day. A cheerleader may well be the first person to tell someone he is creative, generous, joyful, sensitive to feelings, hard-working, attractive. When you encourage like that, you are participating in God's constructive program: "Encourage one another and build each other up. ...Live in peace with each other" (1 Thess. 5:11, 13).

Encouragement is especially needed when someone is trying to change, and change is what pursuing peace is all about. I know. I've been trading in some safe old stress habits for some risky new peace habits. Like a clothing shopper trying on a new suit, I want to know, "How do I look in this?"

It means a lot when my wife tells me, "You handled that differently than you used to, honey. I love you." That's like feeding a dolphin a fish after he does a trick. It is certain he will do another trick!

This positive perspective is not unlike my wife's photographic genius. We use the same camera, but her pictures are prize-winners and mine disappear unmounted into the back of the family album. She took one of her blue-ribbon winners on a gray, misty morning while I was hurrying just to get out of the autumn damp. But Karen saw something I would never have seen—a perfectly formed spider web, glistening with dewdrops. The difference between us is a way of seeing. Where I see a blustery day, she sees beauty.

A praising person has that way of seeing people. In looking each day for the beautiful in those who are close, we begin to replace frustration with peace. We need more cheerleaders.

Brighten the Corner Where You Are

When the grocery clerks went on strike in our area, one unstruck store got everyone else's customers. That was good for the owner, but terrible for the overworked checkout girls. I was determined to make our checker smile. She did and even said thanks for a light moment. I even saw things loosen up once on a grumpy Manhattan elevator, packed to the gills, when someone suggested, "Maybe we should go to an alternate breathing plan."

It is amazing how much difference a person can make who is determined to spread a little joy through his day. There are people who get taken for granted all day—like the gas station attendant. We can "light up his life" just by taking an interest in him—his name is not Phil Erup.

If we live to brighten the corners where we are, folks at home, at the store, at work, or in class will welcome our arrival. Just a smile and a friendly comment can do wonders. If we bring a little peace, we will carry more away.

But peacekeeping is more than just interpersonal. It needs to be *inner*-personal, too. Four of life's peaceful habits reflect on inner attitudes—toward your activities, your failures, your commitments, and your burdens. They pave the way for living at

Peace with Ourselves.

Live Wholeheartedly

The first attitude is rooted in four of the most important words in the Bible. They must be important for they keep turning up! The recurring chant is evident:

- "Love the LORD your God with all your heart" (Deut.

6:5; Mark 12:30).
- "Serve Him with all your heart" (Josh. 22:5).
- "Trust in the LORD with all your heart" (Prov. 3:5).
- "Seek Me with all your heart" (Jer. 29:13).
- "Rejoice with all your heart" (Zeph. 3:14).
- "Whatever you do, work at it with all your heart" (Col. 3:23).

With all your heart—that's the lifestyle of the Bible in four words!

I picture the Olympic runner, straining for the finish line. There is nothing cool or reserved about him. His hair is matted with sweat, his veins are bulging, his lungs are exploding. The gold is not for the cool; it is for the committed! In the Bible, the verbs of life change, but the outlook does not. No matter what the verb, we should go for the gold with all our heart! There is a thrill in living that those who hold back will never know.

There is also deep inner peace in knowing that, whatever the score or the outcome, we have given 100 percent. Whether we work at a lathe, a desk, a computer, or a blackboard, life "turns on" when we work that day with all our hearts. A student's 100-percent attitude will show in careful notes and attention given to the instructor. And in a working world overrun with mediocrity, you *will* be noticed by the people who pay and promote.

Going to church wholeheartedly can make the service you thought was "dead" suddenly have meaning for you. When you learn to *listen* to people without distraction, you will have too many friends to be very lonely again. And an athlete who *plays* with all his heart is welcome on any team.

According to the Bible, we do not pick and choose what is worth our best. It's "whatever you do" (Col. 3:23). And we do not divide our energies—we don't work when we're playing; we don't play when we're working; we don't study when we're praying.

Pressure and anxiety come from violating 100-percent living. Recently a friend told me about some of his employees

whose wives are on the warpath; their husbands are forever
getting home late. They blame the company and the boss for
overworking their men. What they don't know is how hub-
bies mix work and play with extended lunch hours for some
gym time. Combined with ample doses of shooting the
breeze, these men waste as much time as they work. The
result is that they have to make it up at the other end, and
they take the time from their families. If they were at work
when it's time to work, they could readily be family men
when it's time to be family!

Establishing this peaceful habit has upgraded the meaning
of *home* for me. I am learning that sitting in my "Papa's
chair," covered with files and papers, is not being home. In
fact, it is unfair to my children to put right in front of them a
Daddy they cannot have. I am planning my day of late so
that I am really home when I am home—with all my heart.

It helps to pray that way, too. Sometimes I pray more in-
tensively when I get off my seat and on my knees. Or when I
put an arm around the person I am praying with. Or when I
pray with the discipline of allowing a longer time for it. I
wonder if that closet Jesus said we should pray in was not
just for privacy, but to box us in to doing nothing else!
Frankly, I find it boring to pray half-heartedly but it is high-
energy intercession to pray with all our hearts.

As we 100 percent our way through the day, we might well
ask, "Whose gold am I running for?" There is probably no
boss, no church, no coach, no teacher who is consistently
worthy of our total best. When the Bible urges us to "work at
it with all your heart" (Col. 3:23), it also tells us who it is for:

As working for the Lord, not for men,...It is *the Lord Christ* you are
serving (Col. 3:23-24).

Whether sweeping a floor, dictating a letter, or hugging a
child, we inwardly look up and proclaim, "This is for *You!*"
With the Lord as our audience, we can labor, lead, listen,
and love with all our hearts. And whole hearts are peaceful
hearts!

Contain Your Failures

When I hear the fire sirens in our town, I think of all my friends who are volunteer firemen. They tell me that fire-fighting is really a science these days, one based on very fundamental priorities. First, be sure all the people are out of the building. Second, *contain* the damage. Concentrate your resources on keeping the flames from spreading—forget what has already burned.

Failure, like fire, has a tendency to spread. It ravages our confidence, our enthusiasm, our growth, our peace—unless we learn to contain the damage. We can continue to punish ourselves, doubt ourselves, and depress ourselves...or we can choose the freedom of "forgetting what is behind and straining toward what is ahead" (Phil. 3:3).

Forgetting failure is refusing to let yesterday's fall keep me from running full speed today. It is isolating that painful moment, turning the page to today's fresh start. A romantic breakup, a lost position, a spiritual setback, a blowup, a missed goal—the pain of failure, whatever the setting, is real and deep. The pain may last a while, but our performance need not change. The sooner we can be 100-percent-ers again, the faster the wounds will heal.

And some failures aren't failures at all. We have believed the NFL standard of success that comes down to whether you win or lose. In reality, success is how you play the game. In a defeated moment, it is important to ask three decisive questions: "Have I treated people right?" "Have I given my best shot?" "Have I put Christ in the center?" If the answers are all yes, then we *have not failed.*

And if the failure is a real one, we must learn the difference between "I failed" and "I'm a failure." If we fail, we do not change who we are. God forgives and restores at the instant He is asked. It insults His love to keep looking back at what He has erased.

When we learn to contain the fire of failure, yesterday loses its power to take away our peace.

Discuss New Commitments

Not long ago two Amtrak trains were racing full-throttle through New York City. Their trip that morning ended in the sickening sounds of screeching brakes and a deafening head-on crash. Sorting through the mass of twisted metal, investigators asked how these trains got on collision course. The answer was tragically simple. Apparently a signalman had given both trains a green light for the same track!

I visualize the competing commitments of my life in those onrushing trains, all on the same track and ultimately on a collision course. As new opportunities arise, I have a tendency to give the green light one too many times, only to learn later the toll that it will take. It is all too easy to accumulate more responsibilities without seeing the big picture. Sometimes I open up my datebook and exclaim, "How did I *do* this to myself?" I seem to be a slow learner when it comes to remembering that

It is a *trap* for a man to dedicate something rashly/and only later to consider his vows (Prov. 20:25).

I need help! And I need wisdom and objectivity in "considering my vows" *before* I overload the tracks. That's why the Bible purposes an alternative to the stress of regrettable choices:

Plans fail for lack of counsel, but *with many advisers* they succeed (Prov. 15:22).

Get plenty of advice before you flash a red or green light!

The peaceful habit of discussing new commitments begins at home. A major commitment made by any family member affects all the others. If your son or daughter adds an after-school commitment, someone has to drive and, maybe, take their place helping with dinner. If Dad takes a job that requires more travel, he will miss some dates that are very important to the kids. Mom's aerobics or part-time job may leave Junior to come home to an empty house.

Every addition to life has a price tag, much of which is borne by other people. Together, a family may decide that it is worth the cost. But they should decide *together*!

At our house we weigh together the impact of a child's being in marching band and a sport in the same semester. We discuss Mom's vanishing for six weeks to prepare a media presentation. Or Dad's writing a book. It takes cooperation—like each of us disciplining ourselves to write dates on the master family calendar. It is located conveniently underneath the kitchen phone, where most of the "hot opportunities" come along. When we sit down to count the cost, that calendar helps us to see what will or will not work. For me, by the way, family dates—birthdays, concerts, games—go in my datebook first.

It is not only time commitments that can profit from "many advisers"—finances affect everyone, too. Usually saying yes to a major purchase means saying no to some other desires, at least for a while. The family council will probably make a more careful decision than one family member will, especially if it is "his baby."

In many cases, it is wise to discuss new commitments with advisers beyond the family circle. When I was considering an invitation to speak at a conference in South Africa, I consulted our board of directors and my right-hand man about the implications for our local program. Any new direction in our lives should be able to pass the test of objective review by those who will be affected, and a few who will not.

Learn to Laugh

Waiting is a good idea when it comes to any major new commitment. By the time you consult all the important precincts, you will probably make a decision you can live with. If you, like me, are tired of commitments colliding head-on, consultation is a peaceful habit worth working on.

We had just left the grandeur of a twelve-thousand-foot Wyoming peak, and were headed back down into Laramie. As far as we could see across that panorama, it was sunny except right over Laramie. One angry purple patch of storm was obviously coming down on the city. As soon as we drove into town, we were pelted with rain and hail. We felt like we were in the darkness of an eclipse.

Having surveyed the situation from the mountains, we were kept from grumbling about how lousy the rest of the day would be. We knew the storm would soon pass.

Perspective brightens the darkest moments. And learning to laugh is a peace-nurturing habit that helps bring perspective!

Our family was one day away from leaving for a trip when the "storm" hit. We were preparing the house for a young seminary couple who needed a post-honeymoon place to stay. With things to pack scattered everywhere, we discovered that the refrigerator thermostat had malfunctioned, spoiling many dollars' worth of frozen food. As we were tossing the last of it in the garbage can, word came from downstairs that the dryer had died, just when we wanted everything clean.

While I was investigating the dryer, I noticed that sewage had backed up into the basement sink and was slowly forming a swamp all over the floor. It was time to blow up—or laugh. Karen saved us. Standing in the middle of that oozing slime, she harkened back to a recent trip and said, "Welcome to Haiti!" The poverty we had seen there was not funny, but the comparison cracked us up. Because we could laugh, we could handle the mess. In short order, things were back in shape again.

Most of the stresses of life have a lighter side. The secret is learning to look for it. King Solomon believed that, too: "A cheerful heart is good medicine" (Prov. 17:22).

When it comes to living at peace with yourself, remember it is *approach* that has to be perfected: with wholeheartedness; with damage containment; with consultation; with the ability to laugh.

15

Peaceful Working Habits

Adear friend called me the other day. "I need to see you right away," he said soberly. He was facing mounting pressures and important decisions, and needed a buddy. Then my friend proceeded to explain why he had called me. "You have really gotten a new handle on your life in the past few months. I can tell there's a difference."

That was music to my ears. The difference was personal peace, and it was *showing*! Being stressed out is not particularly noticeable these days...it's so common that we think it's normal. But peace *is* noticeable because so few have found it—and when we get near it, we *want* it!

What started in me as a restlessness for something better has grown into a whole new way of living. Like learning to play the piano, it takes practice. And I have discovered that once our personal attitudes toward other people and ourselves are in order, we must learn to live *at peace with our responsibilities and at peace with the unpredictable*. The press of daily demands and the extra weight of life's surprises can, I have discovered, overwhelm even a new you. They are powerful saboteurs of peace. But they can be attacked, captured and rehabilitated. It just takes practice...beginning with four peacemaking approaches to our responsibilities.

Operate in Time Blocks

"Go with the flow" is a nice piece of homespun advice, unless, of course, it is offered on the Niagara River, headed for the Falls. Surrendering to all my swirling responsibilities kept running me up into the rocks. I decided it might be a better idea to try to *control the flow*. I think that is what David had in mind when he prayed, "Teach us to number our days aright, that we may gain a heart of wisdom" (Ps. 90:12).

When we "number our days," we take charge of the time we have. We manage our pressures before they manage us. It begins with the constants in life, the responsibilities that keep recurring. They need to be scheduled as predictably as possible to make room for the unpredictable. A sane schedule is anchored by committed blocks of time; in other words, control everything possible!

We tend to tackle tasks either (1) "when I feel like it" or (2) "when I have to." Since those times come erratically, today's molehill quietly grows into tomorrow's mountain. We end up with six deadlines at once and severely overloaded circuits.

Have you ever noticed that kids will wait forever to practice, to empty the garbage, to start their homework, to clean their rooms? Unfortunately, birthdays don't change that I'll-get-around-to-it-sometime syndrome. We adults are much the same way. Bills wait to get written, calls and letters go unanswered, the laundry mounts up, repairs go unmade. Stress grows in the soil of postponed responsibilities.

Our responsibilities cease flowing uncontrollably when we grab a calendar and *assign them a time*. Set a time to set times. For me, Friday afternoon is the best time to assign time blocks for the coming week.

Remember the *anchor* of your schedule is your quiet centers: your Lord, your marriage partner, your family, your "Sabbath" time. It is around those centers you build in the other commitments needed. In the spaces left, you courageously assign time blocks to all your "knowns." By deciding in advance you eliminate the stress of those predictable tasks chasing you until they catch you.

Honestly, I found it frustrating at first to commit a regular dinner time at home. I always felt more comfortable with an open-ended day, unaware of the uncertainty I was causing my family. Finally realizing that there will always be one more thing to do, I bit the bullet and set a boundary on my office day. The family makes its plans around my commitment now. And I'm starting to enjoy the predictability. Now, a floating arrival time is the occasional *exception*, not the rule.

When we studied *David Copperfield* in high school, I was introduced to the wisdom of an eccentric character named Mr. Micawber. Everywhere he went, he intoned, "Procrastination is the thief of time." He was right! We take our time out of reach of the thief when we assign it in advance.

Plan Your Work

I'm learning that I *save* time when I *take* time to plan my week. At week's end I sit down and make a list of everything that needs doing the following week. In its raw form, it looks overwhelming. But the list becomes manageable as I begin to *prioritize* those responsibilities. A task moves to the top, based on urgency, importance, and whether or not someone else's work is waiting on mine. My next step is to reorganize these tasks by number on my legal pad, starting with the most important down to the least. With list in hand, I can plan to tackle my work with confidence.

When you are looking at a steak bigger than your plate, it's best to approach it in bite-size chunks. The same is true when it's a big project you're facing. "I just don't know where to start," we lament; so we don't. And shrinking time makes the project even bigger! An alternative is starting at the due date and working back to this week, deciding what needs to happen each week. Then, when you make up your "To do" list, you write this week's "chunk" right into your schedule.

One of life's deepest satisfactions, by the way, is crossing things off that "To Do" list. I love it! The discipline keeps me on target in three ways—I work my way down the list in order, as much as possible; work on one thing at a time until it's finished; work my best and quit when it's time to quit.

Today's unfinished work becomes tomorrow's number-one. As well-planned days become well-planned weeks, we begin to taste the sweetness of a life under control.

Consolidate Your Errands

In the days of the Old West, a trip into town was a major event. People would finish their chores, hitch up the team, and set out on the dusty trip there and back. It was special because they did not go often!

Cars, freeways, convenience stores, and shopping malls, on the contrary, seem to encourage lots of trips! We are fractured people, forever running out to get something. Accessibility was meant to simplify our lives, but it has, in fact, complicated them.

Learning to consolidate our errands is a new peaceful habit at our house that has reintroduced us to a refreshing degree of sanity. It all started with our "running list." As we come across something we need, we write instead of run. The grocery, hardware and school needs are recorded until there's a trip's worth. If Karen is picking up our son for an after-school allergy injection, she goes early now and takes the list. Why make four trips when one can do it? If one of us is "going out anyway," we check the roster to see which errand we can incorporate.

At work, most of my desk clutter eventually ends up on my secretary's desk, and she needs to use her time wisely. I have watched appreciatively as she includes her run to the bank and the post office with her trip to lunch. The successful salesman plans his route carefully because he knows that time is money. Salesman or not, a person who values time will plan his route, too.

Consolidating errands is really a mindset, a thought process that faithfully asks, "How can I save steps?" and "Is this trip really necessary?" You can tell you're regaining control when you reach for the doorknob and the car keys—and then put them—away. It's way more rewarding than another trip to 7-11!

Do the Difficult First

Damocles may have been the original insomniac. The ancient Greeks said his bed was situated right under a sword, delicately dangling by a single thread. Since those days folks have been referring to "The Sword of Damocles" as anything unpleasant that hangs over one's head!

Every person with responsibility has a job that haunts him just like that sword. Because we dread it, we postpone it...it doesn't go away. That pending "dirty work" drains our energies and keeps us on edge. The sooner we bite the bullet and get "the job" done, the sooner we can relax.

For me it is worth getting up early to have an hour alone in the office. That golden hour sets the pace for the day. Inevitably, there is something unpleasant in front of me: a stack of mail, a difficult letter to write, a personnel problem to solve. It takes all the self-control and courage I can muster sometimes to start with the task I most want to delay. But when I do, the relief and freedom I feel can energize my work for the rest of the day! (It's second only to checking off my "To Do" list!)

Every setting has in it jobs we avoid—cleaning the garage, studying a least understood subject, defrosting the refrigerator, grading papers, filling out reports. If we run from these tough tasks, they will chase us wherever we go. As long as it is on our minds, dirty work produces stress. Once it is done and off our minds, its hold is broken.

That's why it is a peaceful habit to do the difficult first. Why keep looking at that dangling sword, when we can simply cut it down?

In a world bursting both with need and opportunity, shrinking from responsibility is cowardly and stressful.

When we control the flow instead of going with it, we have room for the next challenge. And for the unexpected. Our peaceful habits grow to help us live calmly with *life's unpredictables*.

Leave Space for "Murphy"

Our living room was totally dark and jammed with teenagers all over the floor. My unsuspecting daughter got out her key, opened the front door and mumbled something about nobody's answering her knock. Suddenly the room blazed with lights and twenty kids screamed the magic word: *"Surprise!"*

Some surprises add spice to life—parties, weekend getaways, gifts. But not everything that jumps out of the dark yelling "Surprise!" is fun.

An overheated car is a surprise; so is a traffic jam, a forgotten bill, or being locked out of the house. And even those surprises seem trivial when compared with the unexpected layoff, a serious illness, a painful accident or the devastating death of someone you love.

Handling your responsibilities peacefully is a little easier—there you are dealing with the "knowns" of your life. Preparation for living at peace with the unpredictable means preparing for the unknown...and deciding in advance how you will handle it. The comparatively "safe" surprises of life have been aptly explained in the famous Murphy's Law: "Anything that can go wrong *will* go wrong." For peace to last, you have to make it a habit to leave space for Murphy.

Unfortunately, busy people act as if they never heard of Murphy. They schedule wall-to-wall days in which nothing had better go wrong. This tendency to overschedule is an open invitation to severe stress. I know, I have been an expert at it.

Does this sound familiar? I schedule a staff appointment exactly thirty minutes after the anticipated ending of a business lunch. The restaurant is, of course, exactly a half-hour from the office. There is absolutely no time for that businessman to pour out an unexpected personal heartache—or for construction on the Interstate. Then, allowing exactly sixty minutes for that staff appointment, I schedule a counseling session. If unanticipated discussion arises in meeting with my colleague, we just borrow some time from the counselee's hour.

This "domino effect" makes us tense, along with everyone around us. A reputation can grow around our unpredictability. Because you were late, your appointment comes late the next time, thus augmenting the domino collapse in your jam-packed day.

Overscheduling is also a by-product of the "just-one-more-thing" syndrome. In an effort to reduce a little pressure, before we leave we try to squeeze in just one more phone call, one more shopping stop, one more load of laundry. We race to everything. And this kind of overheated living sets off alarm systems all through our bodies.

Even a neighborhood Bible study can suffer from overscheduling. When Ruth got a reputation for coming late (she was making one more bed!), other ladies got tired of wasting their time. They came late, expecting to arrive just as Ruth did. When Ruth came on time one week, she found many of the ladies not there, so (you guessed it!), she made *more* beds before coming the next time. The women finally decided to start on time, no matter what.

Plan your day to leave some time unscheduled—you just cannot schedule as if nothing will go wrong! Management experts recommend that busy executives leave unscheduled anywhere from 20 percent to 40 percent of their time. All busy people have to leave room for surprises! Wise planners put padding between their appointments, and have open time into which they can throw the unexpected.

Overscheduling is only part of the Murphy problem. It is aggravated by underestimating. Leading a Sunday school class appears to be just a one-hour slot in the week. But where does preparation time come? If one meeting is right on top of another, when do we catch our breath and prepare for the next one? We simply underestimate both the preparation and follow-through for our commitments.

The alternative to underestimating is *anticipating*. That kind of thinking kept my sailing friend, Dave, dry. He was enjoying an idyllic sailing afternoon on Long Island Sound. His only contact with the real world was the Yankees game coming through on his radio.

Dave's ears perked up when he heard the sportscaster suddenly announce, "Folks, everything is suddenly blowing all over this stadium. It was completely calm a minute ago, but now a strong wind is blowing like everything here!" Dave immediately lowered his sail. Ten minutes later he was relaxing on his deck, watching as one sailboat after another plopped over sideways in the Sound. Dave anticipated the problem—and therefore had one less problem to solve.

Murphy's Law really is a fact! We compound our pressures when we plan as if we have *everything* under control. Pollyanna planning like that is bound to backfire.

Leaving space for Murphy limits the damage he can do. When you open up your life a little bit, the surprises don't sink you.

Rely on Eagle Power

About 4:00 A.M. in my college dormitory, I discovered "eagle power." Working all the way across the city, I would often roll in from the buses and subways around 11:00 P.M. I did what homework I could on the bus, but I could not start most of it until I got back to my room. That led to many all-nighters—and a special need for energy to make it through the next day.

In those exhausted moments, the remarkable words of the prophet Isaiah touched me:

He gives strength to the weary,
and increases the power of the weak.
Even youths grow tired and weary,
and young men stumble and fall;
but those who hope in the LORD

will *renew their strength*.
They will *soar on wings* like eagles;
they will *run and not grow weary*,
they will walk and not be faint (Isa. 40:29-31).

The prophet was telling me that there is *special power available when I am unable to depend on the usual sources of strength*! Like the Rocky Mountain updrafts lifting the eagle, I could soar even on tired wings.

I have felt totally depleted many times since those all-nighters. When fatigue is the result of a God-honoring day, we can reach up for eagle power. In fact, He is gracious enough to energize us supernaturally even when we are victims of our own unwise choices.

I don't believe God meant for us to run full throttle all the time and then collapse into His arms, crying, "eagle!" But there are those moments when there are people to care for, tasks to complete...and nothing left to give. If we try to crank out a little more personal resource, we may eventually burn out. Those who reach up for eagle power will find they can fly!

I cannot explain this supernatural surge of second wind. I only know that peace and power are there for the asking when ours is all used up.

Capture Your Environment

Whatever personal prison may be holding you back right now, it is probably not as bleak as the infamous "Hanoi Hilton." That was the name the American prisoners of war gave to their prison camp during the Vietnam War. Most of these incarcerated flyers were there three to five years, some as long as nine years.

Those endless months of monotony, loneliness, and torture would be enough to drive any man crazy. Instead, these flyers survived with an incredible sense of balance and sanity. Their captors had planned on their prisoners' demise, but the Americans turned prison time into an opportunity for personal development.

Some learned foreign languages. Others learned to play imaginary musical instruments by using memories of strings and keyboards—enough to come home as talented instrumentalists. One group put together a Bible from a composite of all the verses they could remember, and proceeded to commit that mini-Bible to memory. One officer played golf in his imagination for years, and returned to the USA as a tournament-level competitor. The prisoners had made the "Hanoi Hilton" into the University of North Vietnam.

Any prison can be transformed that way, whether it is the prison of a fixed income, of living alone or personal pain. The secret of this peaceful habit is to *capture your environment ...don't let your environment capture you!*

I have watched my wife do just that as she has recovered from hepatitis. When you take an active, "looked to" woman and put her in a bed for six months, you might expect some justifiable discouragement and frustration. To give into those negatives would have been letting her environment capture her. Instead she has ministered to everyone close by, capturing her environment instead. She has loaded up her room with Christian books, teaching tapes, seminar notes—and her Bible and notebook. Karen has dedicated this quiet time to what she calls "deepening her roots." The glow we can see in her is a radiant testimony to her personal growth. An extended time of rest and solitude could be a prison of self-pity...or the undisturbed spiritual feast she has made it.

That was the spirit of Joseph when he was imprisoned for a crime he did not commit. The Book of Genesis tells us that he went through that dark place looking for sad faces he could cheer up. When Paul and Silas were locked up unjustly...

About midnight Paul and Silas were *praying* and *singing* hymns to God, and the other prisoners were listening to them (Acts 16:25).

No prison could ever hold Paul's spirit. He used his time to write much of the New Testament!

There are times in our lives that we perceive to be in-between times, and we can easily squander them waiting for the next big event. We are waiting "until" we get a better job, get married, get out of this dinky apartment, get well or "until the Lord takes me home." But we were created to bloom where we are...to act as if we are going to be there for a long time.

When the captive Jews were looking toward seventy years of Babylonian internment, they were tempted to put everything on hold. Instead, God commanded them to: "Build houses and settle down; plant gardens and eat what they produce...seek the peace and prosperity of the city to which I have carried you" (Jer. 29:5, 7).

There are still "gardens" to be planted—in any of life's seemingly unpleasant surprises. There are experiences to enjoy that you will never afford after you're married—decorative touches that make that one room something special...people to care for in the place where God has "carried" you.

Our environment looks a lot brighter when we look for ways to make the most of it. We are practicing peace in the surprises of life.

Cultivate Flexibility

I have constructed some impressive plans in life, some of which have been executed without a hitch. How rewarding! Then there are those surprises—the complications blew the plan apart. If our peace is to survive those maddening moments, we need to cultivate flexibility.

I always consider *my* plan as Plan A...until God lets me know that He has a higher plan. When He changes our course, we can fight it...or relax and enjoy the ride. How often I have had to learn, sometimes like a pouting child, that

In his heart a man plans his course,
but the LORD determines his steps (Prov. 16:9).

I was set for the writing of this book. I had set aside the

times and places where I would go to work on it. Everything looked great until Karen got sick and needed my help. It's as though I was being tested on the very theme I was addressing! (God often does that.)

At first, I resisted like the old stressful me was used to doing. But my pursuit of peace was teaching me something about enjoying God's surprises. I prayed, took Karen for her blood test, hugged the kids, and plugged in the typewriter.

The Master Author had a much better story line than what I had written for myself. God wanted me to draw my inspiration, not from a little cabin in the woods, but from a real-life test of the peace I was writing about! As a result, I have found a far deeper, more realistic peace than my Plan B would ever have provided. I believe what I am writing about more than ever!

When people are inflexible, they invite great stress in the surprises of life. When they practice flexibility, they invite great peace...peace rooted in that deep confidence that God's redirections are never detours. They are instead the best route to the best destination.

When I was a kid, I had a "cowlick" in my hair; it refused to lie down. It might have been cute on a little boy, but I'm glad I don't have it now. My mother kept laying on the water and the Vaseline to let that hair know who was boss. She told me she was training that cowlick. It worked. That stubborn hair quit standing up. (In fact, some of it has quit growing!)

Training works. After years of "standing up," I am trying to learn how to rest. My training revolves around the conscious, deliberate *practicing* of these peaceful new habits.

This lifestyle is definitely taking hold at our house. When it's time for a discussion...an errand...or adjustment...a commitment, we keep asking each other the same question:

"Are we pursuing peace?"

The dictionary tells us that a habit is "an acquired behavior pattern regularly followed until it has become almost involuntary." It is exciting to discover that peaceful responses can actually become "almost involuntary." To become a habit, peace just has to be "regularly followed."

16

His Way in the Storm

Our two boys love history. But they hate tours. In fact, they have managed to make the word *tour* into two very long syllables. "Daddy," they moan pitifully, "are we going on a tooooooo-ur?" When I assured them one summer morning we were going to see a working early-American town, not just costumed ladies telling about old buildings, they consented. Cautiously.

The craftsmen made the place come alive. The blacksmith worked his magic with fire and iron, the miller showed us how a waterwheel and some wheat equals flour, and the potter made us forget any leftover impressions of a "tooooooo-ur."

His skill was almost hypnotic.

He sat at his wheel, rhythmically turning the shaft with his feet. In a nearby corner were shapeless, seemingly worthless gray blobs of clay. One of those former blobs was now the focus of all his attention. With practiced fingers the potter was working that clay upward into a smooth and shapely vase.

The potter's shack was cramped, too small for all the people crowded in to watch on that hot day. Eventually, the crowd left. But our kids wanted to stay. They had noticed two shelves of finished vases, one on either side of the potter. With childlike innocence one young son reached out to touch.

"Careful!" the craftsman exclaimed. "Please don't touch the pottery on that shelf. You'll ruin it." Then he surprised us when he said, "Why don't you touch the ones on the other shelf?" Needless to say, we were curious as to why some vases could be touched and not others.

Glancing at the "do-not-touch" shelf, he explained, "These haven't been fired yet." The potter told us then that there was more to masterpieces than just making blobs into beautiful shapes. If he stopped at that point, they would quickly be marred and misshapen. Without the fire, the potter's work is still beautiful, but too fragile.

The other vases could be touched because they had twice been baked in his kiln at temperatures of more than 2,000 degrees! "The fire makes the clay firm and strong," our host concluded. "Fire makes the beauty last."

That was the trigger. My thoughts raced to Peter's words:

All kinds of trials...have come so that your faith—of greater worth than gold, which perishes even though *refined by fire*—may be proved genuine (1 Pet. 1:6-7).

Both Peter and the potter were talking to me about a *fire that increases the value of something precious*. Having spent most of my adult years in an oven—a pressure cooker, to be exact—I knew about fire. Much of it could be traced to my over-heated schedule and over-committed lifestyle. That heat was my own fault.

But there is another fire that comes, not from me, but from the Master Potter. There is, to be sure, a heat that burns, and another heat that *beautifies*.

The Lessons of Stress

From that first day that I discovered, "Seek peace and pursue it" (Ps. 34:14), in the Scriptures, I hoped that my life would slow down. It hasn't, but I have. By removing some roots of my restlessness, I have performed surgery on the stress that comes *from* me. By attacking stress centers in my life, I am managing the stress that's coming *at* me...and there is still plenty left! That's because there is *supposed* to be.

What keeps pushing on me is the heavenly stress that is *for* me the heat that improves, strengthens, and beautifies.

Personal peace is not the elimination of stress. If we live without pressure, we are as fragile as that potter's unfired vase. God has been skillfully reshaping me on His wheel, making a "blob" into something far more valuable. But that workmanship needs fire to make it firm and strong.

In pursuing peace, I am trying to eliminate *the stress that I cause* and to control that which *others cause*. What's left is *the stress that God Himself either causes or allows*. Peace-living resists self-induced stress but grows from God-produced stress.

If the pressure is taken off a piece of coal, there will be no diamond. Removing that irritating grain of sand from an oyster's tummy means having no pearl. Protecting an apple tree from the pain of the pruning knife results in little fruit. Pressure, irritation, and pain can be tools to develop people, too.

It's the wrong kind of pressure that can crush or weaken or kill. That is where my "gerbil-wheel" life had created an overload. Even with much of that unloaded now, my days still get crunched with plenty of demands, changes, and frustrations. While the weight is as much as ever, it just doesn't seem as heavy. God may send a load—but never an overload.

As my stress-weary heart has followed the word *peace* through the Bible, I uncovered this perspective on my pressures:

Endure hardship as discipline; God is treating you as sons.... No discipline seems pleasant at the time, but painful. Later on, however, it produces *a harvest of righteousness and peace* for those who have been trained by it (Heb. 12:7, 11).

There it is! Stress that *contributes* to our peace! Hardship here is defined as training. But if we are not looking for the trainer's lesson in the problem, we get only the pain and miss the peace. When a peace-pursuer understands he is in training rather than in trouble, he can relax even under fire. Knowing that peace will come from this pain doesn't make the pain any more enjoyable, but you handle it calmly.

Frankly I almost lost my personal peace before it was even a month old. My "showdown with stress" had come at the end of the summer. I came away from my turning point with a fresh sense of hope, sensing I had finally regained control. I had made specific commitments to my Lord, my wife, my children, and my work—commitments based on the biblical description of a peaceful life.

That's when everything started to unravel.

I expected fall to be a circus as usual, getting three children acclimated in three different schools, managing the high-energy startup of another school year in youth ministry, a heavy schedule of speaking and meetings.

I entered the fall fray joyful and expectant, confident. I had learned to practice peace. I did *not* expect the avalanche on top of the circus. It started late in September at a local high school football game. I was grabbed by a friend who blurted out, "I think your son has a broken arm." It took only a look at Doug to confirm the bad news.

I will never forget the scene that followed in the emergency room. Because both bones were broken and twisted, the doctor had to probe and push and pull for a long time. Doug was brave, but his pain was almost unbearable. Strangely, in a way only a parent could understand, so was mine. When we finally got home, Karen and I agreed that we felt totally depleted—as if *we* had each broken an arm.

The emotional struggle lasted a lot longer than the physical pain. A broken arm may not rate very high on a chart of human suffering, but it is a heavy burden for an athletic twelve-year-old. All of his fall sports dreams were shattered with his arm. His natural self-consciousness about beginning junior high was complicated by four months in a cast. Doug's favorite seasons—Halloween through Thanksgiving, Christmas, and New Year's—evaporated as his friends ran hard and he laid low. When the doctor later announced that the bones were healing crooked, we realized this battle could actually last for years, not months. There were tremors in my new peace.

That broken arm turned out to be only the opening shot in a barrage of new tensions. The night Karen and I returned from Haiti, she was seized with a severe gastrointestinal attack. Unable to move, Karen had to be rushed to the hospital by ambulance before our bags were even unpacked. Her pain was so severe, our family doctor stayed most of the night with us. It was the second time in two weeks I had stood in this same emergency room, watching someone I love suffer.

This was to be followed by Karen's dangerous attack of phlebitis, forcing her to bed when we were running full speed together to finish a major project. By the time the hepatitis put her in bed for six months, we either had to laugh or cry. We did some of each. Just for good measure, we threw in a week in the hospital for our daughter, too. The tremors were beginning to register higher on the Richter scale.

With things at home up for grabs, it would have helped if things at work were stable. They weren't. It was at this same time that we faced a severe cash crisis that I mentioned before. It threatened to paralyze us. Our people were not complaining, but they were not being paid on time. Simultaneously, some unresolved personnel conflicts surfaced, threatening to pull us apart. The long meetings that ensued led to new stresses of some major reorganization. The frosting came with our landlord's notice—he had sold our office building and we would have to move!

By now, I had a major "peacequake" reeling inside me. Just when I was trying to simplify my life, it got more complicated. I found myself on my knees asking, "God, if You want me to pursue personal peace, why is all this happening? You aren't even giving me a chance!"

Actually, a chance for peace is exactly what God *was* giving me. These upheavals were forcing me to rearrange misplaced priorities, some I would never have seen any other way. Unhealthy dependencies were being broken, as "asking Ron" was becoming more difficult. I was unintentionally less available because of the fires I was fighting. And I was driven closer to my Lord than ever before. Since He is the Ultimate Source of peace, I began to taste that "peace of God, which transcends all understanding" (Phil. 4:7).

God allowed me to be caught in an avalanche of friendly stress. He was helping me, driving me, to reorganize my life around saner expectations.

And the tests had not taken my peace...they had confirmed it. God was speaking through this whirlwind to say, "This peace of Mine is stronger than you thought!"

Father-Filtered

There is another stress that God does not send, but one He *allows*. In Old Testament times, Job exemplifies this dramatically. The Bible makes it clear that all his losses and suffering were Satan's idea, calculated to disillusion his faith in God. Yet even the devil cannot bring pressure and pain without God's permission!

A unique behind-the-scenes look at spiritual warfare emerges from Job's predicament. Satan could not touch Job until God OK'd it. Satan approached God, asking to go beyond the "hedge around him and his household" (Job 1:10). The Lord gave a conditional yes when He answered, "Very well, then, everything he has is in your hands, but on the man himself do not lay a finger" (Job 1:12).

Job's glue through this personal holocaust was a faith that declared, "Shall we accept good from God, and not trouble?...The Lord gave and the Lord has taken away;/ may the name of the Lord be praised" (Job 2:10; 1:21).

His analysis was, at best, only partially right. Actually, the devil had "taken away" and sent the "trouble." But Job trusted in a Father who knows what is best for His children, and that he had to OK these trials somewhere along the way.

Job's troubles make ours look like pin pricks. Still, I have found myself asking during our recent avalanches, "Is God

trying to build us or is Satan trying to bury us?" Since that
question is virtually unanswerable, I have decided to ask a
better question, "How can God use this?" If this pressure
could not train me, the Coach would not allow it. Our problems look much less terrifying when we realize they are
"Father-filtered." That filtering is guaranteed in promises
such as,

God is faithful; He will *not let you* be tempted beyond what you can bear
(1 Cor. 10:13).

In other words, nothing can enter the life of God's child
without His signature. His approval is based on what we can
bear. He will allow me to be pushed to the building point,
but not the breaking point. Like a weight lifter, too much
weight would crush us. But greater weight than we lifted before is needed to make us stronger. Only the Lord knows the
difference, and He filters every additional load.

Everywhere the apostle Paul traveled, he was relentlessly
tormented by his unnamed "thorn in my flesh" (2 Cor.
12:7). He identified its source as "a messenger of Satan" (2
Cor. 12:7). In spite of the devilish origin of his trouble, *he
looked for the lesson*—a reason his Father would allow it. Paul
concluded his thorn was sent "To keep me from becoming
conceited....that Christ's power may rest on me" (2 Cor.
12:7, 9).

That same pressured preacher also looked for the Lord in
His trouble and sensed His saying, "My grace is sufficient
for you, for My power is made perfect in weakness" (2 Cor.
12:9).

That perspective is the margin of emotional survival. It
enabled Paul to win in the worst moments of his life. "We
are hard pressed on every side, but not crushed; perplexed,
but not in despair; persecuted, but not abandoned; struck
down, but not destroyed" (2 Cor. 4:8-9).

Survival Skills

In all the hoopla of the 1984 Summer Olympics in Los

Angeles, one tragic casualty was generally overlooked!
Boomer didn't make it. In the extravagant opening ceremo-
nies, a bald eagle named Boomer was scheduled to soar into
the Coliseum to the strains of "America the Beautiful." Unfortunately, Boomer was unable to show up for his performance. Three days before the Olympics opened, Boomer
died—of stress, they said.

I guess even an eagle can tell when things are out of hand.
People pressure was just too much for the old bird. He knew
how to survive the dangers of the wilderness but not the
stresses of civilization.

We can sympathize with poor Boomer...we all have those
crushing moments when we feel like we're dying of stress.
Recent medical research tells us that many people are literally killed by stress. For the rest of us who feel the punishment of emotional dying, survival skills become crucial.

To establish quiet centers and peaceful habits gives us precious resource for inner peace. When we attack the roots of
stress in us and the chronic stress centers around us, we
make room for the friendly stress that will always be there.
But even with that plan for peace in place, there is one important item of unfinished business. How do we handle "the
rest of the mess"...the "circumstances beyond our control"?

There are important answers in the account of the most violent storm experienced in the Bible. Acts 27 describes the
savage nor'easter that threatened the ship transporting Paul
to trial in Rome.

They lost all control of their circumstances—yet they survived. And locked inside this storm-tossed story are the *four
skills* we need to survive the unavoidable storms of stress.

Get Rid of the Cargo You Don't Need

Luke the author of Acts explains the first survival skill in
this way: "We took such a violent battering from the storm
that the next day they began to *throw the cargo overboard*....with their own hands" (Acts 27:18-19).

If someone had suggested to the captain of the ship upon departure that the cargo, the ship's tackle—and maybe even his favorite chair—were going overboard, he probably would have burned their ears with his reply. Yet when the storm hit, they decided they could do without some items they once were sure they needed!

If we are going to handle our own personal nor'easters, we will have to *get rid of the cargo we do not need*. Of course, it sometimes takes a storm to make us even consider letting go.

Some of our "extra cargo" may be bad things we have accumulated like barnacles: a compromising relationship, deepening debt, a growing obsession with money, an entangling sinful habit, a critical attitude—things we hang onto until a storm exposes how they are sinking us.

There is good cargo, too, that may have to be jettisoned. We tend to accumulate involvements that, taken separately, are each neutral—even helpful. But, taken together, they are just too much.

A storm is our chance to change...when the rough weather subsides, we can return to the same overloaded or wrongly loaded lifestyle. That in turn could set the stage for an even bigger storm.

If you want to survive your personal "hurricane," evaluate extra cargo, and get rid of it before it sinks you, one way or another.

Get Busy with the Things that Really Matter

Luke tells us that "Hurricane Paul" lasted two weeks! Then an angel appeared to Paul in the middle of the night. Paul's visitor introduced a second survival skill for a storm. The apostle announced this message to the crew:

"Not one of you will be lost; only the ship will be destroyed. Last night an angel of the God whose I am and whom I serve stood beside me and said,...'God has graciously given you the lives of all who sail with you' " (Acts 27:22-24).

In essence, the angel had simply reminded Paul, "The

ship doesn't matter. Only the people do." To survive a storm you *get busy with the things that really matter...* and those "things" are usually *people!*

With all the pressures to achieve and accomplish, the people we love can slowly get pushed to the corners of our lives.

Neglect is not intentional—weeds grow in our garden, not because we plant them, but because we forget them. Many a man leaves a wife or a child in his dust as he speeds toward his career goals. Many a woman slowly vanishes from the most important moments of her loved ones as she loses herself in a job, a social circle, a religious responsibility. Coworkers or employees can become functions instead of people with needs.

Without realizing it, we let those close to us become simply dispensers of information, transportation, hugs, money, or services. It usually takes a storm to restore our values.

In the pursuit of peace, the "ship"—the project, the schedule, the deadline, the organization, the budget—may be lost on the rocks. That is costly, but it's OK. It is our *people* we cannot afford to lose. If the storm blows you back to them, you have all you really need. You can always find another ship!

Get Desperate with God

Our faith tends to be cool, calm, and collected, until a crisis clobbers us. Then we go from our feet to our knees, and God becomes more than Someone who "helps" us: He is our only hope.

Luke apparently spoke for himself and Paul, too, when he said, "We finally gave up all hope of being saved" (Acts 27:20).

That is probably why the visiting angel greeted Paul by announcing, "Do not be afraid, Paul" (Acts 27:24).

I am glad for that glimpse of the apostle's humanity. He is on such a pedestal in my mind that I would expect to find him standing bravely in the bow of the boat, like George Washington crossing the Delaware. Instead, Paul seems to be as terrified as everyone else, and as desperate. In his desperation he is met by "the God whose I am and whom I serve" (Acts 27:23).

Paul models for us a third survival skill in a storm—getting desperate with God. When the bottom drops out, it is easy to get desperate. The sailors on Paul's ship sensed they were headed for the rocks. So...

In an attempt to escape from the ship, the sailors let the lifeboat down into the sea....Then Paul said, "Unless these men stay with the ship, you cannot be saved." So the soldiers cut the ropes that held the lifeboat and let it fall away (Acts 27:30-32).

Often our panic makes us reach for a lifeboat instead of the Lord. My lifeboats have usually just made bigger messes. I have hired the wrong people, spent unwisely, cut programs too soon, pushed people I love too hard. A storm can make you panic or make you pray.

It is when our points of reference disappear like the sailors' stars that we learn what prayer really means. Stripped of any possibility of self-rescue, we throw ourselves on the Lord. Our praying is not controlled, predictable, third person; we finally open our religious hand and let God fill it with something supernatural.

At points in your life with Him, God will strip you of all other resources, leaving you only Himself. Then you discover, in the words of a wise old saint:

You never know Jesus is all you need until Jesus is all you've got.

And then there is peace, no matter how long the storm lasts. In the words of King David, you can proclaim:

When anxiety was great within me, your consolation brought me to my soul (Ps. 94:19).

Get Back to a Healthy Routine

When the boat is headed for the rocks, lunch can wait. Yet as Paul's ship was about to go aground, he urged the crew to eat. "For the last fourteen days," he said, "you have been in constant suspense and have gone without food...Now I urge you to take some food. You need it to survive" (Acts 27:33-34).

Paul advocates here a fourth survival skill in a storm—*getting back to a healthy routine.* When a strong disturbance batters our ship, our daily routines are usually the first things thrown overboard. In reality, the heavier the pressure, the more important it is to guard our sources of strength.

When anyone starts to miss sleep, meals, and breaks, he starts sinking. Quiet centers tend to be neglected when we start cutting corners. More than ever, we have to fight for that quality time with our Lord, our lovers, and little ones. Those healthy routines are what keep us strong on both sunny and stormy days.

Blown Where You Belong

There's a line from an old hymn that beautifully interprets the storms we face...

Clouds arise and tempests blow by order from Thy throne.

When God orders up a tempest in my life, it is because a change is needed. Usually, the storm is not the real issue—not from God's viewpoint. It is an imbalance that has developed in my priorities, a dislocation so subtle that I can't even see it until turbulence gets my attention.

It is in storm that I literally get blown back in balance. I am learning not to throw that wonderful new peace overboard when my ship spins out of control. It is, instead, time to get rid of the cargo I do not need...get busy with the things that really matter...get desperate with God...and get back to a healthy routine. God has provided that positive strategy for weathering the storms of friendly stress.

The account of Hurricane Paul ends with a thrilling postscript. Luke records that the tempest finally blew them aground on the island of Malta. One look at a map reveals what was really happening in the midst of that raging crisis at sea. Malta sits right off the southern coast of Italy, the ship's original destination! The whole time they thought they were out of control, they were *right on course*!

Centuries before, the ancient Jewish prophet Nahum said it all in a simple sentence: "The Lord has *His way* in the whirlwind and the storm" (Nah. 1:3).

Our plans may be interrupted by storms; God's plans never are. In fact, that storm is *part* of His plan. If we don't abandon ship, the winds of God will blow us right where we belong—no matter how off course we feel.

Coping Isn't Enough

Nancy's "glass of stress" is full and overflowing. Wedged between the demands of single parenting, a rebellious son, and managing office, she has just about had it. When she heard I was writing about peace and stress, she said, "Oh, I'm reading something right now about how to cope with stress. I hope I find out in time!"

Most of us pressure cooker people would, like Nancy, consider it success just to cope with our stress. But after years of coping, I have decided that coping is not enough.

According to the dictionary, to cope is "to struggle or contend on fairly even terms." That sounds like treading water but never getting to shore! Since my stress-saturated life did not drown me, I guess I was coping. But just keeping our heads above water leaves us vulnerable to any big wave that comes along.

When I made a commitment to go after peace, I wanted to learn to *conquer* stress, not just to cope with it. Stress was too often dredging up my dark side... subverting our family life... shuffling sane priorities. I hungered for a peace that would break its grip.

I found it in a promise in the Bible that has been tested by two millennia of believers. The apostle Paul had the credentials to pen the words; turbulence and upheaval had been a way of life for him. Just before the promise he lists every major disturbance in the human experience:

Trouble...hardship...persecution...famine...nakedness
...danger...sword...death (Rom. 8:35,36).

Then, with this catalog of life's storms in mind, he pro-
claims:

In all these things we are *more than conquerors* through Him who loved us
(Rom. 8:37).

If we can be more than conquerors in the stresses of life,
why should we settle for coping?

The difference between coping and conquering seems to
be those two little words—"through Him." Without them,
this is just another inspiring way to say, "Think positively."
Real personal peace is not the result of positive thinking.

Peace is ultimately a Person. The ancient Jewish prophets
called Him "the Prince of Peace." When Jesus came, the
Christmas angels promised He would be a Savior whose saving would bring peace. When He left, He promised:

"Peace I leave with you; My peace I give you" (John 14:27).

His servant Paul summed it up when he reminded us:

He came and preached to you who were far away and peace to those
who were near (Eph. 2:17).

Then, in six simple words, he spoke the prescription for
peace:

For He Himself is our peace (Eph. 2:14).

I was one of those Paul described as "those who were
near." Years ago, I had recognized that the war in my heart
was really a battle with God. I realized that I could not have
Christ's peace until He was my Prince. Opening the hands
that had so tightly gripped the steering wheel of my life, I let
Jesus Christ drive.

Since we were made to live for the God who made us, everything else is out of place until we find Him. And He can
only be found at the Cross where His Son paid the bill for

our war against God. Whether we have rejected God, or simply neglected Him, the result is the same—a life He made and paid for, lived without Him. Upon our invitation, He enters our lives...bringing His peace.

Since my personal visit to Jesus' cross, I knew the Person who is peace. Through the most turbulent stress seasons, I have been unsinkable, as Paul said "Through Him who loved us." His pressure on the inside has always been greater than the pressure on the outside.

But, for so long, I have been something much less than "more than conqueror." My complicated lifestyle had allowed too many other hands on that steering wheel. I wasn't crashing, but I was swerving. Then the prison cell door swung open, and my Rescuer said, "Seek peace and pursue it."

I have been ever since. This book is a chronicle of the choices and changes that followed. The peace I hungered for has been there since Christ came in. But I was like a man with an inexhaustible bank account who wasn't writing many checks on it. The poverty, the pressure of my life was waiting for peace to come instead of going after it.

Inner peace is the *natural condition* of the heart in which Christ lives. I just need to quit blocking and sabotaging the supply lines.

In a sense, my search for peace ends where it began. Years ago I came to Christ for peace. Years later, I am learning to enjoy it by discovering Him more deeply than ever before. The pursuit of peace is ultimately the pursuit of a *Person*.

The gales of stress have blown me to the Prince of Peace. And just as Paul was carried to God's destination by that nor'easter, He may be using the storms of your life to drive you to Him.

If the load you are carrying seems too heavy for you, it is because you were never meant to carry it alone. Coping may well be touch-and-go struggle, conquering, totally out of your reach. Stress is eroding even your ability to cope.

That moment of extremity is His opportunity. Strangely

enough, you may be closer to peace than you have ever been, and the stress of your life has carried you there. We stand tired of fighting... and Jesus quietly whispers:

"Come to Me, you who are weary and burdened, and *I will give you rest*" (Matt. 11:28).

Strong and proud, we don't feel the need, even though it is just as urgent then. But battered and wounded by years of battle, we *know* we need help—the rest. That's when our hand reaches for His. Peace *is* a Person... and peace rooted in Him can triumphantly stand any test.

Corrie ten Boom testified to that from the "greatest hell man could create"—the Nazi concentration camps of World War II. She and her dear sister, Betsie, paid the price for hiding Jews in the attic of their home in Holland. Through torture, humiliation, and pain, they turned to the Christ who lived in them—and tested His peace. Their witness was backed by the credentials of a suffering few of us have ever known.

Betsie died in that concentration camp; Corrie was released as a result of a clerical error. In Betsie's dying hours, she spoke a message that Corrie would carry around the world for nearly forty years. Betsie said,

Tell them that *there is no pit so deep but that God's love is deeper still.*

Corrie and her sister had tasted what it means to be "more than conquerors through Him who loved us." The peace that Christ brings is that strong.

If my stress makes me hungry for His peace, then it has driven me home. The storm has blown us into the Harbor that we have looked for all our lives.

NOTES

NOTES

NOTES

NOTES

NOTES

NOTES

NOTES

NOTES

NOTES

NOTES